AMERICANS IN AFRICA
1865-1900

HOOVER INSTITUTION STUDIES: 17

AMERICANS IN AFRICA 1865-1900

CLARENCE CLENDENEN

ROBERT COLLINS

PETER DUIGNAN

The Hoover Institution
on War, Revolution, and Peace
Stanford University, 1966

Preface

The Hoover Institution Studies are monographs designed as building blocks for the use of scholars of many disciplines concerned with many different parts of the world. These building blocks may be complete in themselves, or they may be treated as material to be incorporated later into a larger structure. We therefore invite comments, criticisms, and suggestions from interested scholars for change or improvement as the Studies appear.

The present monograph is the third in a series which began with *The United States and the African Slave Trade, 1619–1862* (Hoover Institution, 1963, 72 pp.) and *Americans in Black Africa up to 1865* (Hoover Institution, 1964, 109 pp.), and it forms part of a larger general investigation on United States involvement in Africa.

Our purpose has been to set down in broad strokes a general picture of United States activity in Africa. We have concentrated on the American aspect of African affairs and have said little about African reactions to American merchants, missionaries, and explorers. The study is based primarily on printed sources (except for several doctoral dissertations and the private papers of a number of men) and represents a synthesis of historical scholarship. Much of the information, however, was mined from American memoirs and autobiographies, missionary reports, journals, and government dispatches. Some of these sources have thus far been neglected by African, American, and European scholars. It is our hope that others will be encouraged to work in the area and unearth further facts. Given the lack of previous published research on America's role in Africa (two notable exceptions are the work of Norman Bennett of Boston University and George Shepperson of Edinburgh University), we have had to concentrate on narrative rather than on interpretation or analysis.

Many friends and colleagues read and criticized the manuscript: Professor Thomas Bailey of Stanford University, Dr. Lewis Gann of the Hoover Institution, Dr. Alan Booth of Ohio University, Dr. George Brooks of Indiana University, Dr. Norman Bennett of Boston University, Dr. John Peterson of Kalamazoo University, and Dr. J. G. St. Clair Drake of Roosevelt University.

The authors take full responsibility for any errors that remain, and the opinions and judgments expressed here are theirs alone.

Clarence Clendenen
Robert Collins
Peter Duignan

Contents

AMERICANS IN AFRICA
1865-1900

The United States and Africa up to 1865

Few Americans, until very recent times, have been aware that the vast continent of Africa, second largest land mass in the world, was more than a geographical curiosity, more than the home of strange animals and seemingly primitive men. They have been unaware that Africa and the United States, in innumerable ways, have had (and continue to have) a vital impact upon each other. Completely ignored, usually, is the fact that 10 percent of the people of the United States are descended from African ancestry. Because the United States took no part in the partition of Africa and never acquired an African colonial empire, the political and economic interests of the United States in the continent have been almost entirely overlooked by historians and other scholars. Hence, the achievements of numerous Americans in the development of Africa remain largely unknown. It is in the hope of presenting the main outlines of the role played by Americans and their government in Africa that the writers have undertaken this series of studies. In addition, they desire to point out that much unexamined source material for the study of Africa is held in the United States and to encourage students to delve more deeply into this material.

Although the history of contacts between the people of western Europe and Africa goes back to ancient times, the first significant European encounters did not take place until the Portuguese explorers pushed down the west coast of the continent in the fifteenth and sixteenth centuries. In addition to the geographical information they acquired, the Portuguese noted that the African was an adaptable worker who could labor and survive under almost any kind of condition. With the expansion of European settlements in the Americas, vast amounts of labor were needed—labor which could not be supplied from Europe or from the native Indian population of the newly

11

opened continents across the Atlantic. Thus the slave trade was born, a commerce about which few people felt any qualms at the time and into which the African coastal peoples entered wholeheartedly. For several hundred years the principal export of Africa consisted of men and women—hands to do the necessary labor on the plantations of South America, of the West Indies, and finally of the English colonies on the mainland of North America.

As is well known to students of United States colonial history, the first Negro slaves were sold at Jamestown in 1619, brought there by a Dutch privateer that had probably looted them from a Portuguese or Spanish slave ship. This incident constituted the first step in the relationship that developed between the English colonies and Africa. Negro slavery, however, was not firmly established for many years. Although the planters of the southern colonies needed labor, they lacked the credit or cash necessary for the purchase of slaves. It was not until they achieved a fairly high degree of prosperity and produced a large volume of money crops that it was possible for them to import Negro slaves in considerable numbers. In Virginia in 1655, for example, nearly half a century after the colony was founded, there were only three hundred Negro slaves out of a total population of several thousand people. But the closing years of the seventeenth century and the opening decades of the eighteenth saw a change in economic and social conditions, and Negro slavery became firmly fixed in the institutions of North America.

Negro slavery achieved importance in the southern colonies with the development and extension of a plantation economy—agriculture on a large scale, as distinguished from the relatively small "family farm." Slave trade became important, too, in the northern colonies, where climatic and geographical conditions produced a commercial, rather than an agrarian, economy. This trade guaranteed a market for such New England products as lumber, salt, and fish; rum distilleries operated to provide the medium of exchange demanded by African slave dealers; vessels built in New England shipyards and manned by New England sailors carried the products from which profits flowed back to New England farmers, fishermen, carpenters, barrelmakers, and scores of other craftsmen. It was the slave trade which kept colonial business operating smoothly.

Certain places became especially important. Ships from Boston, Salem, and New York were conspicuous, but pre-eminence was attained in the eighteenth century by the small colony of Rhode Island. Newport, along with London, Bristol, and Liverpool, became known as one of the great slave-trading ports of the world. Virginia and South Carolina provided the principal continental markets for slaves —in these two southern colonies the plantation economy developed most quickly and extensively. It should be noted, however, that from the standpoint of the slave trade as a whole continental North America was always a minor market. By far the greater part of the unfortunate African migrants to the New World went to the West Indies and South America, particularly Brazil.

In the latter part of the eighteenth century, with the spread of the ideas and ideals of the Enlightenment and the religious revival, opposition to slavery and the slave trade began to develop throughout the Western world, particularly in Great Britain and the United States. After the successful outcome of the Revolutionary War, such ideas spread rapidly in the United States, and within a few years all the northern states abolished slavery within their borders and forbade their citizens to engage in the trade, while men everywhere looked forward to the end of slavery. Southern states too hoped that slavery would gradually disappear. In the Constitutional Convention, which framed the fundamental law for the new nation, there was no opposition to a provision fixing a date when Congress could forbid the trade and prohibit further importation of slaves from Africa.

In Great Britain, a judicial decision in 1772 effectively destroyed slavery within the kingdom. Thereupon, led by such men as Granville Sharp and William Wilberforce, a concentrated attack was made upon the trade; almost simultaneously, in 1807, the Parliament of Great Britain and the Congress of the United States outlawed the transatlantic traffic in men.

Before this took place, however, the mechanical genius of a young Yankee schoolmaster, Eli Whitney, and the rise of the industrialized cotton mills in England gave a new lease on life to the supposedly dying institution by making it immensely profitable. Only the volume of available cheap labor appeared to limit the growing capacity of the English cotton mills to consume raw cotton and the ability of the

13

American South to produce it after the invention of the cotton gin. Thus were the efforts of the British government and the Royal Navy to stamp out the slave trade thwarted; great riches resulted from the few successful slaving voyages, although many slavers lost their investment. Efforts by the United States to cooperate in putting an end to the procession of slave ships across the Atlantic were handicapped by the bitterness of the domestic controversy on slavery, but all evidence indicates that the number of slaves imported directly into the country after 1807 was small. The Brazilian and Cuban markets were still open and flourishing.

Efforts by Great Britain to obtain the cooperation of the United States in ending the transatlantic slave trade were complicated and hampered by the traditional attitude of the United States toward Britain's previously asserted "right of search." But without it positive identification of a slave ship was impossible. The right of search had been one of the prime causes of the War of 1812, and the United States, until after the outbreak of the Civil War, grimly refused to concede the right to stop and search any ship flying the American flag. Even so staunch an enemy of slavery as John Quincy Adams violently opposed such an "outrage" against American national dignity. Moreover, Great Britain, after two major wars, had come to be regarded by most Americans as the traditional enemy, intent upon destroying American commercial competition, with the slave trade a ready excuse and the British African squadron the weapon.

There were years of complex and often somewhat acrimonious diplomatic negotiations, punctuated by numerous "incidents" on the African coast in which the Royal Navy seized American ships. Finally, in 1842, as a result of the Webster-Ashburton Treaty, an American naval squadron was stationed on the west coast of Africa, where it remained until after the opening of the Civil War. The operations of the United States Navy in suppressing the slave trade have been mentioned disparagingly by several writers. It has been charged that the government in Washington was deliberately indifferent towards fulfilling its treaty obligations, or that southern naval officers turned a blind eye towards slave ships, or that the various southerners who served as Secretary of the Navy hampered the antislave patrol. One recent writer, for example, says categorically, "It is clear that there was a deliberate attempt on the part of the Navy Department to comply only technically with the Treaty" by sending a small number of heavily overgunned ships to the African coast and that the United States rarely had more than five ships as compared with some twenty-five maintained by the British and French.[1] The writer says further that frequently the ships sent to Africa were the culls of the United States fleet and were wholly unsuited to their task.

Admittedly the U.S. naval ships sent to Africa were unsuited to chasing slavers and in some instances were so old as to be unseaworthy. But only a casual glance is needed to show that the naval authorities were limited by what they actually had. Such criticism fails to take into account the fact that the United States of the 1840's was not a great naval power. In 1843, the year in which the African Squadron came into being, the entire strength of the United States Navy consisted of seventy-six vessels of all sizes, classes, and descriptions. Eleven of these (several of which were uncompleted but nevertheless carried on the list) were ponderous ships of the line, which no one would have considered sending to Africa. There were fifteen frigates, almost equally inappropriate. Ten vessels were storeships or were in use as receiving ships at various ports. Of the five small steamers which the United States Navy had at this time, one was permanently landlocked in the Great Lakes and the others were unfit for a transatlantic voyage. In 1843, the available ships were spread over the whole world, nine in American waters, four or five in Africa, five in the Mediterranean, five on the Brazilian coast, six in the Pacific, two in the East Indies (with replacements en route), and most of the remainder either "in mothballs" (as were nearly all the large vessels) or under repair and refit.[2] The Royal Navy, on the other hand, included over 250 vessels in active commission, not counting those that were laid up or unmanned.[3]

The inability of the United States to proceed more actively on the

---

[1] Alan R. Booth, "The United States African Squadron, 1843–1861," in Jeffrey Butler (ed.), *Boston University Papers in African History,* I (Boston, 1964), 100.

[2] Department of the Navy, *Report of the Secretary of the Navy,* November 25, 1843, pp. 472–475.

[3] House of Commons, *Session Papers,* December 3, 1857–August 2, 1858, Vol. XXXIX, pp. 1–11.

African coast was summarized succinctly by Lord Napier, the British Minister at Washington, in a dispatch to Lord Aberdeen on April 19, 1858: "The American navy is ill supplied with light vessels, and it may be doubted whether Congress would sanction any pecuniary appropriation for the purpose indicated."[4] A moment of mental arithmetic will show that the United States Navy, proportionally, made as heavy a contribution as the Royal Navy.

A more serious allegation is that southern officers in the African Squadron deliberately avoided capturing slavers and that their instructions were so framed by southern Secretaries of the Navy that it would be impossible for them to make such captures. Such a view is not borne out by the records or by the instructions themselves. Two officers who were most active and most successful in pursuing and capturing suspects were both southerners. No more than in the British or any other modern navy have the officers of the United States Navy allowed personal feelings to influence their obedience to lawful orders and their enforcement of them. Although instructions to the African Squadron from Washington stressed that the American ships were to protect lawful American commerce and to use all means to promote and further it, nowhere was it either stated or implied that they were to neglect due attention to the slave trade. On the contrary, instructions were specific and definite and left no room for doubt. It might be added that even among proslavery southerners there was no considerable body of opinion favoring the slave trade, in spite of the vehemence of a few extremists in the late 1850's.[5] The handful of ships, all that were available from year to year, cruised continually in the areas where slavers might be encountered. To complain that they were ineffective ignores the fact that the criminal takes care not to practice his profession when an officer is in the vicinity.

Incomplete records show that in the period between 1837 and 1862 the pitifully inadequate American navy accounted for at least

---

[4] "Correspondence with the United States' Government on the Question of the Right of Visit; Presented to Both Houses of Parliament by Command of Her Majesty," in House of Commons, *Session Papers,* December 3, 1857–August 2, 1858, Vol. XXXIX.

[5] See Ronald Takaki, "The Movement to Reopen the African Slave Trade in South Carolina," *South Carolina Historical Magazine,* LXVI (1965), 38–54.

107 slave ships.[6] In addition, on several occasions it joined forces with the Royal Navy in sending expeditions into Africa's creeks and estuaries to "cut out" hidden slave ships and destroy the barracoons. If the American squadron on the African coast was not the spectacular success the present age might wish, the basic fault lies not with the navy but with the American people who would never have consented to expenditure of the sums necessary to build special vessels and with the American courts which made conviction of a captured slaver virtually impossible.

Closely related to the slave trade and slavery were the activities of the American Colonization Society on the western coast of Africa. Many philanthropic people, both northern and southern, were deeply concerned in the early nineteenth century by the plight of the free Negroes of the United States. It was widely believed that repatriating them to their ancestral continent would benefit them and at the same time solve the problems their presence entailed. There were slave-owners, too, who were opposed to the institution of slavery, but they believed that it would be inhumane to free their slaves and subject them to the lack of care and to the indifference and discrimination which seemed the free Negro's lot. Added to such well-meaning slave-owners were those who saw in the free Negro a threat to their own safety and property. As a result a large and highly influential segment of public opinion in the United States favored establishing somewhere (preferably in Africa) a colony to which the free Negroes and freed slaves could be sent. In 1818, the American Colonization Society sent agents to Africa to locate a site for such a colony. Congress enacted a law providing that slaves rescued by American naval vessels be liberated at the colony established by the Society, and President Monroe determined to establish a depot there for receiving such slaves.

The Society, meanwhile, had organized the first group of returnees to Africa. When financial difficulties developed, the United States government, under a friendly arrangement, seized the ship and took over the operation. The colony encountered almost insuperable difficulties. With the cooperation and help of both American and Royal navies, however, and some assistance from the neighboring British

---

[6] See Warren S. Howard, *American Slavers and the Federal Law, 1837–1862* (Berkeley and Los Angeles, 1963), Appendix A, pp. 213–223.

colony of Sierra Leone (also a refuge for free Negroes), the colony survived. For several years it existed as a political anomaly. The United States government denied any authority or official connection but did in fact extend a certain amount of both diplomatic support and naval protection. In 1847, by arrangement with the American Colonization Society, the settlement proclaimed itself an independent and sovereign country with the name of Liberia. Recognition was at once extended by Great Britain, France, and other European nations. For reasons growing out of domestic politics, the United States withheld formal recognition until the outbreak of the Civil War, when Washington was freed of social domination by slaveowners.

The grim events of 1861 in the United States changed abruptly the situation regarding the slave trade. The American squadron was withdrawn from African waters to reinforce the fleets blockading the rebellious slave states in America. Quietly, the United States government retreated from its former position and suggested that British war vessels investigate and take appropriate action toward suspected slavers flying the American flag. Although, as mentioned before, there is no evidence that any considerable number of slaves were imported into the United States directly, the illicit trade had unquestionably been furthered by the protection of the American flag—protection which vanished with the war and its outcome. The Atlantic slave trade did not finally disappear until the abolition of slavery in Brazil and Cuba, but in its last few years of existence it was negligible. A few hundreds of slaves were furtively smuggled across the ocean where before tens of thousands had been transported openly. While the trade flourished, however, the effects upon the society, economy, and development of the United States were so evident that any detailed mention becomes unnecessary.

Slave trade was the major feature of contacts between the United States and Africa before the Civil War, but it was by no means the sum total of such relations. Slaves for export and rum and items in payment for slaves did not comprise the entire commerce between the United States and that continent, nor did they account for all the contacts between the peoples of the two regions. As the nineteenth century progressed, some Americans were deeply concerned about the salvation of African souls; others desired to learn the secrets of the continent which had so long been hidden from the Western world.

American commerce with Africa, outside the slave trade, started early in the annals of the English colonies, but it is impossible to fix the exact time or to determine its extent. Until the trade in slaves was outlawed, it was as legitimate a form of commerce as any other, and such records as have survived seem to indicate that ships from America went to Africa looking for anything that was marketable—slaves, ivory, gold dust, dyewood, whatever the African trader had to offer. New England became a shipping and commercial area in the early years of its development, and there are records of occasional voyages to the west coast of Africa and to the Indian Ocean and Madagascar beginning in 1645. Unfortunately for the historian, American ships sailed under the British flag previous to the Revolutionary War, and it is difficult now to distinguish them and their activities from those of other British vessels in African and Indian Ocean waters.

After the Revolutionary War, American merchants and shipowners began extending their activities throughout the world. In this they were fortuitously aided by the outbreak of the wars of the French Revolution and of Napoleon in Europe. For a number of years European trading posts on the West African coast were virtually dependent upon American shipping and American products for their very existence. The War of 1812 temporarily interrupted American trade, but when peace returned to the Western world in 1815, Americans again appeared in Africa in numbers and at the same time began to extend their commercial activities up the eastern coast of the continent. Vessels from New England, principally from the little port of Salem, finally achieved a near monopoly of the commerce of the huge empire of the Sultan of Muscat, who transferred himself and his capital to the East African island of Zanzibar. Here American merchants became predominant, and in the two decades before the Civil War ivory, hides, gum copal, and other African products for the expanding factories of New England were exchanged for cotton goods, gunpowder, hardware, and a thousand and one items needed by the Africans. Americans remained conspicuous in Zanzibar and the commerce of East Africa until after the Civil War, which, for a variety of reasons, initiated the decline of direct American foreign commerce and the virtual end of the American merchant marine.

In West Africa, American merchants and traders did not achieve the pre-eminence they gained at Zanzibar, but they built up large and profitable businesses and, like their compatriots on the east coast, were prominent in African economy until after the Civil War.

In both Europe and America, the first decades of the nineteenth century saw a revival of the urge to spread the Christian gospel that had characterized early Christianity. The movement led to the formation of numerous missionary organizations and the sending of missionaries to all parts of the world. Since Africa was almost totally pagan or Moslem, it received proper Christian attention. Even before the Revolutionary War a mission to Africa was projected by Samuel Hopkins, of Newport, Rhode Island, in which educated free Negroes were to be the missionaries. Nothing came of it, however, and the first missionaries from the United States to the Dark Continent went in connection with the American Colonization Society's colony that became Liberia. In 1833, the American Board of Commissioners for Foreign Missions, an interdenominational organization, sent the first group who went for the purpose of evangelizing the indigenous peoples. Settled originally near Cape Palmas, they were constrained, in a few years, because of the terrible death rate at that place to transfer themselves and establish their mission at the mouth of the Gabon River. Here, in spite of difficulties and dangers caused by French imperialistic activities, the mission proved permanent.

The American Board, simultaneously with sending missionaries to West Africa, sent a group to South Africa, upon the invitation of Dr. John Philip, superintendent in South Africa of the London Missionary Society. There also the Americans had their difficulties and dangers, becoming involved in the wars between the Zulus and the restless Boer farmers. Nevertheless, they were eventually able to establish their missions so firmly that they became influential media in the evangelization of the region, and the American missionaries earned an honored place in the esteem of Africans, Boers, and Britons.

Although the two instances mentioned are probably the most conspicuous examples of American missionary effort in Africa, they were far from being the only ones. American Roman Catholics endeavored to found missions for their faith in West Africa, only to be defeated, as the Protestants were, by the endemic disease which the medical knowledge of the time was unable to conquer. In the early 1850's, the Reverend Thomas Jefferson Bowen, representing the Southern Baptist Church, explored Nigeria with a view to founding missions of his church in Yorubaland. He spent months in investigation and exploration, took a prominent part in defeating a slave-raiding invasion from a neighboring area, and won the affection and esteem of the people among whom he worked to the point that his mission proved a success. He himself, however, was compelled to return to America, his health shattered.

At the time of the American Revolution, inner Africa was completely unknown to the rest of the world. The intellectual curiosity that characterized the era led to many efforts to penetrate beyond the coastal fringes and solve the continent's mysteries—among these the source, or sources, of the Nile and the course and end of the Niger. (The "Oil Rivers" were not yet identified as the rivers of the Niger delta.) An adventurous young American, John Ledyard, who had sailed as a member of one of Captain Cook's expeditions into the Pacific, volunteered to assist the newly founded Association for Promoting the Discovery of the Interior Parts of Africa, especially in trying to solve the problem of the Niger. But he died of disease in Cairo before his journey was fairly started. Another American, Archibald Robbins, of Connecticut, shipwrecked on the African coast, captured by Arabs, spent three years as a slave and after his ransom was able to describe in detail places as yet unseen by Europeans. Probably most noteworthy of all was Paul Belloni du Chaillu, French born but a naturalized American citizen. In the mid-part of the century, for purely scientific purposes, he explored vast areas in Central Africa. His announcement of the existence of a giant species of ape, the gorilla, was greeted with disbelief by European armchair savants, and his statements on geographical matters were denied by the same authorities. Du Chaillu happened to be right. His most astonishing discovery, however, was a race of pygmies, of whom the world had had no previous knowledge.

The American flag was never hoisted over African soil as a symbol of sovereignty, but Americans as individuals held their own among those who opened Africa to the world and helped dispel the many mysteries of the huge continent.

21

CHAPTER 1

The Vanishing Flag

In West Africa, as in other parts of the continent, the era following the American Civil War was one in which American trade declined almost to the vanishing point. At the outbreak of the war, however, the American trader was a conspicuous figure from Senegal to Angola; the American flag floated over scores of small craft anchoring off many African villages and in rivers, inlets, and tidal estuaries along thousands of miles of coast line. A network of consuls, vice-consuls, and consular and commercial agents fostered the interests and watched over the trade of the United States all along the African coast.

In contrast, a report by the British consul general at Tangier in the early 1890's showed that during a period when more than a thousand vessels entered that port, there was among them not a single American ship.[1] Nevertheless, the organization by which the State Department endeavored to safeguard and extend American commerce in Africa remained virtually intact. This included seven paid consuls and a score or more of honorary consular agents. But the pay of the honorary agents, derived from their fees, was admitted by the Department to be no pay at all, and the total value of American trade with tropical Africa was less than that of trade with the Kingdom of Hawaii. For commercial information on Africa, the United States was almost entirely dependent upon the reports of British officials.[2]

The causes for the decline of direct commerce between the United States and West Africa were the same as those which brought about

---

[1] Department of State, Bureau of Statistics, *Commercial Relations of the United States with Foreign Countries during the Years 1894 and 1895* (Washington, 1896), I, 17. This series is hereafter cited as *Commercial Relations*.

[2] *Commercial Relations, 1895–1896*, pp. 58, 59, 62, 71, 98, 1009–1011. In the period 1895–1896, the total value of imports and exports between the United States and Hawaii was $33,831,815.17; the total trade with all of Africa amounted to $25,027,679.

the decay of commerce with other parts of the continent. First and foremost was the Civil War itself, which struck the first heavy blow against American foreign commerce. On March 1, 1862, the acting consul at Bathurst reported: "The unfortunate differences in the United States have, during the last twelve months, severely affected the importation of American goods, which has fallen off nearly one-third."[3] For four years American shops and factories devoted their major effort to war production, with very little surplus left for export. Erstwhile farmers, mechanics, and factory workers were in the trenches before Petersburg or were shouldering muskets in Tennessee or Georgia. The sailors and shipmasters who had carried the American flag and American products to the limits of the Seven Seas were manning the blockading fleet that strangled the South. Many of the schooners and brigs that had borne American products to the coasts of Africa were plodding up and down the American coast, bearing coal, hay, lumber, blankets, and barrels of beef to the blockading ships and the Union garrisons from Matamoros to the mouth of the James. American merchants who maintained African connections found it difficult to procure the goods their African customers wanted, and for most of the products of Africa there was no immediate market in the United States. To keep their businesses alive, American merchants frequently had to purchase goods in Europe and transport them to Africa in British, French, or Hanseatic ships. Moreover, the ravages of Confederate cruisers which were capturing and destroying large numbers of American ships all over the world placed a direct premium upon trading under a European flag. The *Alabama* burned Yankee vessels in African waters; the *Shenandoah*, in the North Pacific, destroyed the American whaling fleet that had hunted along the coasts of Africa.

Yet there were some exceptions. The demands of the Union armies for boots and shoes gave a stimulus to the importation of hides into the United States; consequently, trade between the United States and South Africa, instead of declining, increased as a direct result of the war. The trade in hides picked up sporadically in other African areas

---

[3] Congress, Senate, *Letter of the Secretary of State, Transmitting a Report on the Commercial Relations of the United States with Foreign Countries for the Year Ended September 30, 1862*, 37th Cong., 3d sess., S. Exec. Doc. (1863), p. 155.

as well. Surprising increases occurred for short periods in the trade with Senegal and the Gambia.

Nevertheless, it is correct to say that American foreign commerce started on the downgrade during the Civil War. The downward movement was accelerated by a technological change that began about the middle of the century—the world-wide transition from sail to steam. Steam transportation proved to be cheaper than sail and had the additional advantage of regular schedules made possible by relative independence of winds and weather. Although American trade with Africa held up fairly well during the 1870's, the appearance of European steamships on the African coast marked the doom of the American merchant or trader who depended upon a small sailing vessel. His merchandise could not compete with goods brought from Europe by transportation that cost a fraction of what he had to pay. As early as 1872 there were complaints from dissatisfied customers on the Gold Coast that American goods were procurable from Europe as cheaply as from America.[4]

The effects of steam navigation upon West African trade and commerce were especially noticeable first on the Gold Coast, where steamship service was introduced in 1852. Merchants in that region began to deal directly with Great Britain and thus broke the near monopoly which had been maintained for years by a handful of London firms. A second steamship line in 1869 brought transportation costs still lower, and in the cutthroat competition which followed, Americans were eventually frozen out.[5]

The decline in American trade with Africa, started by the Civil War and by changes in transportation, was continued by the westward expansion of the American people in the decades following the war. American thought and effort were directed toward the Far West. Foreign commerce became a minor activity as farmers, entrepreneurs, investors, and adventurers swarmed into the economic and social vacuum of the Great Plains, the Rocky Mountains, and the Pacific Coast and began to develop farms, mines, industries, and transportation in those regions. By and large, for the entire period from the

---

[4] George E. Brooks, "American Legitimate Trade with West Africa, 1789–1914" (unpublished Ph.D. dissertation, Boston University, 1962), p. 186.

[5] *Ibid.*, pp. 185–186.

24

Civil War to the end of the century, American capital found such abundant opportunities within the boundaries of the United States that there was relatively little incentive to seek opportunities and profits abroad. It was a period of isolationism, economic as well as political and diplomatic, during which almost no serious attempt was made to regain the position which American merchants had once held in the commerce of the world.

As the British Empire extended its sway over various African territories, a deliberate effort seems to have been made to eliminate American competition. On the Gold Coast, for example, the small number of American traders, already handicapped by shipping and transportation, found themselves further beset by discriminatory ad valorem duties. Revision of the colony's tariff schedules in 1876 and 1877 caused duties to fall most heavily on the two American products that were still imported into Africa in large quantities—rum and tobacco.[6]

In other parts of West Africa the picture was similar. In Sierra Leone, in 1872, the duty on tobacco was raised from one and a half pence per pound to four pence; on spirits, to two shillings per gallon. Smuggling (to which the Americans were not at all averse) increased sharply but could not offset the decline in trade. Beginning in 1873, for example, American purchases of raw hides, which had been the major American import from Sierra Leone, began to drop off. Within a few years American trade was no longer of any importance in the colony's economic life.[7]

In French West Africa, the United States established a consulate at Gorée in 1883. Like many of the others, the consul was unsalaried and was expected to reimburse himself from the fees of his office. Any possible hope that this appointment might stimulate American trade with the French colonies was to be disappointed, for by the early 1890's the application of the new French tariffs (Méline tariff) and other conditions finally squeezed out the Americans. The United States consul at Gorée did not bother to submit an annual report, and in 1895 the State Department noted that the trade of France and

---

[6] *Ibid.*, pp. 224, 233, 237.
[7] In 1883 goods from the United States constituted only about 9 percent of Sierra Leone's imports. See *Commercial Relations, 1882–1883*, pp. 90–93.

Great Britain with Senegal was, "for all practical purposes," the sum total of the commerce of the country. In short, American trade with French West Africa had ceased to exist.[8]

In Angola, where American interests had once been so extensive that American merchants found it necessary to maintain permanent establishments at Ambriz and Loanda, the story of vanishing American commerce was similar. The last United States consul posted at Loanda reported in 1892: "Since the closing of the United States naval store at Loanda . . . no American traders have settled in Angola; but since 1881 several American missionaries [have become] an important factor in the population."[9]

The decline of direct trade did not mean that no American goods were sold or traded to West African customers or that no African products found their way to the factories and consumers of the United States. But these items were no longer carried across the Atlantic in American vessels, and in most instances they were noted in the inventories of the British, French, or German traders who had supplanted the Yankees. The United States was still the world's greatest tobacco producer, and Africans consumed enormous quantities of tobacco; the production of kerosene (coal oil) was almost an American monopoly, and kerosene quickly replaced native animal and vegetable oils in the lamps and under the cooking pots of Africa. In spite of the fact that German gin was cheap, many Africans continued to prefer the American rum upon which their alcoholic tastes had been formed.

American trade with Africa (excepting South Africa) remained an unimportant item in the commerce of the United States during the latter years of the nineteenth century. Few American merchants or firms were sufficiently interested to endeavor to regain the position that Americans once held in African economy. American businessmen forgot how to conduct business in Africa and with Africans, and casual attempts to maintain customary American mercantile practices were foredoomed to failure. It was not until the 1920's that Americans again attained a position of importance in West African commerce.

---

[8] Information furnished in a personal communication by Mr. George Brooks, November 24, 1964. See also *Commercial Relations, 1894–1895*, I, 19.

[9] *Commercial Relations, 1894–1895*, I, 23–24. See also Congress, House, *Report on Commercial Relations of the United States with All Foreign Nations*, 34th Cong., 1st sess., H.R. Exec. Doc. 47 (1857), p. 476.

CHAPTER 2

The Lamb and the Wolves

The Civil War marks a dividing point in nearly all aspects of American history and development. It was true in the record of Afro-American relationships, and nowhere was the change more distinct than in the relations between the United States and its African protégé, Liberia. Although the United States had actually fathered the African republic and maintained an informal protectorate over it, no formal diplomatic recognition had ever been extended to the new state. Recognition would have entailed the presence of Liberian diplomats in Washington and Liberian consuls in the major ports of the country. That Negro diplomats, some of whom might even have been former slaves, should rub shoulders with slave-owning aristocrats had seemed unthinkable to the American "Establishment" of the day.

Despite the lack of formal recognition, the United States government maintained relations of a sort with the Liberian government.[1] Thus in 1861 the Secretary of the Interior noted that more than 4,500 Africans, rescued from slave ships, had been landed in Liberia in a period of little more than a year, "under contract with the Government of Liberia."[2] But the bombardment of Fort Sumter and the exodus of slaveholding southerners from Washington changed the situation radically. President Lincoln stated in his message to Congress on December 3, 1861: "If any good reason exists why we should persevere longer in withholding our recognition of the independence

---

[1] For continuity of the narrative, this paragraph and the next five paragraphs are repeated, with minor changes, from Clarence C. Clendenen and Peter Duignan, *Americans in Black Africa up to 1865* (Stanford, Calif., 1964), pp. 55–57.

[2] Congress, Senate, "Report of the Secretary of the Interior," *Senate Executive Document 1* (1861), 37th Cong., 2d sess., p. 453. See also Congress, House, *Letter from the Secretary of the Interior . . . as to Contracts for Returning and Subsistence of Captured Africans,* 37th Cong., 2d sess., H.R. Exec. Doc. 12 (1862), which gives details omitted from the first-mentioned report.

and sovereignty of Hayti and Liberia, I am unable to discern it."[3]

In the press of wartime business, Congress did not act upon the President's recommendation immediately, but in June, 1862, finally gave its approval to recognition of the two Negro republics. Shortly after, John Seys took his post at Monrovia as United States consul, and the President was able to report in his annual message for 1862 that an advantageous treaty had been concluded with Liberia and was awaiting the Senate's confirmation.[4]

John Seys, the first representative of the United States to be accredited formally to Liberia, was one of those men whose quiet influence has been deeply important but is too often overlooked by historians. A native of the British West Indies and a convert early in life to Methodism, he spent several years in the ministry and in missionary activities in Trinidad and other West Indian islands. Shortly after coming to the United States, he was appointed to a missionary station among the Oneida Indians. His energy, sincerity, and tact gained converts to the point that in a few months he was able to report that he had an interracial church composed of a hundred Indians, seven whites, and one Negro. Meanwhile, the newly established Methodist mission in Liberia was engaging the attention of the church's authorities, and on April 7, 1834, upon the recommendation of Bishop Elijah Hedding, the Board of Managers appointed Seys to that station. He arrived in Liberia on October 18, 1834. Except for a few short visits to the United States, he remained in Liberia until 1841, when he felt compelled to resign owing to difficulties with Governor Thomas Buchanan and to his wife's failing health. The next year, however, on learning that Liberia was without a Methodist missionary, Seys volunteered to return. In 1845 his wife's ill health again forced him to give up his post, and he returned to America. But he was far from through with Liberia. In 1858 he was appointed United States Government Agent in Liberia for Freedmen, and, as

---

[3] Congress, Senate, "Message of the President, December 3, 1861," *Senate Executive Document 1* (1861), 37th Cong., 2d sess., p. 6.

[4] Congress, House, *Message of the President, December 1, 1862,* 37th Cong., 3d sess., H.R. Exec. Doc. 1 (1863), p. 5; Congress, Senate, *Letter of the Secretary of State, Transmitting a Report on the Commercial Relations of the United States with Foreign Countries for the Year Ended September 30, 1862,* 37th Cong., 3d sess., S. Exec. Doc. (1863), p. 221.

already noted, was the first consul of the United States in Africa.[5]

Early in 1863 the President appointed John J. Henry Commissioner and Consul General to Liberia, but Henry resigned before taking up his post. In his stead, Abraham Hanson formally presented credentials to the President of Liberia on February 25, 1864. Unfortunately, Hanson succumbed to an African fever two years later, whereupon the office was tendered to John Seys, who took up the duties of Minister Resident and Consul General in the fall of 1866.[6]

Formal recognition and the designation of diplomatic representatives placed relationships between Liberia and the United States on a regular basis. Before recognition, however, the Liberian government drew moral strength, and sometimes a degree of physical aid, from the friendly interest of the parent country. The presence of the American naval squadron in African waters enabled the struggling Liberian government to act decisively against slaving establishments; the occasional visit of an American warship was a definite object lesson to African tribes, as in 1852, when the sudden appearance of the U.S.S. *John Adams* had a very quieting effect upon the chiefs at Grand Bassa. The withdrawal of American ships during the Civil War deprived the Liberian government of this moral and physical aid, and for several years the Liberian authorities found themselves handicapped in their efforts to extend their authority—and sometimes even to maintain themselves in places they already held.

One of Minister Seys's main interests was the securing of a suitable armed vessel from the United States to enable the Liberian government to suppress slaving and maintain order among the coastal people. As early as 1864, in his last annual message, President Lincoln had urged that he be given authority to sell to Liberia a gunboat no longer needed by the United States Navy. In 1866 Congress approved such a sale, on terms that would have made the craft practically a

---

[5] Wade Crawford Barclay, *Early American Methodism, 1769–1844 (History of Methodist Missions,* Part I; New York, 1949–1950), I, 282, 285, 301, 310, 338, 340–343, 344; II, 147.

[6] Information furnished by Mr. Herman Kahn, Assistant Archivist for Civil Archives, National Archives, Washington, D.C., in a letter to the authors, July 11, 1962. It is not clear why the first representatives to Liberia (and Haiti as well) were designated Commissioners, instead of Ministers. Seys was the first to hold the title of Minister.

gift. Unfortunately, however, none of the surplus war vessels was suitable—they were either too small for African service or too large for the scanty resources of the Liberian government.

Two other intergovernmental matters that marked the first years of formal diplomatic relations between Liberia and the United States were the arrangement of a postal convention and the supervision of the immigrants who continued to arrive in Liberia from the United States in small numbers. Their transportation and supplies for the voyage to Africa were still furnished by the United States government. Caring for the immigrants after their arrival in Africa and watching after the interests of the government he represented seem to have been the American Minister's major activities.[7] Seys resigned in 1870, at the age of seventy-one years, after a lifetime devoted to the arduous service of his church and his adopted country. He died in 1872.

During the time that Seys represented the United States in Liberia, the unofficial and personal interest in the Negro republic on the part of numerous Americans was exemplified in the exploration of the hinterland by Benjamin J. K. Anderson, a young American-Liberian. In response to the desire of Liberian President D. B. Warner to learn more about the regions that abutted upon the country, Anderson volunteered his services. Backed financially by two New York philanthropists, Henry M. Schieffelin and Caleb Swan, Anderson left Monrovia on February 14, 1868, accompanied only by a few carriers and canoemen. His mission was to penetrate as far as possible into the interior and, if feasible, to visit Musardu, the so-called capital of the West Mandingoes, a place probably never seen by any Liberian or other outsider.

Anderson made his dangerous trip alone except for his canoemen and carriers; terrified by tales of the perils of the country and the unspeakable cruelties of the Mandingoes, other Liberians refused to join him. Ten months later, on December 7, he arrived at Musardu, after repeated delays caused by desertions among his carriers and by continuous attempts to make him turn back. His life was threat-

---

[7] Department of State, *Papers Relating to the Foreign Relations of the United States, 1867–1868*, pp. 318–319, 326–331. This series is hereafter cited as *Foreign Relations*.

ened more than once, but by a combination of tact, cool determination, and an occasional threat to use his firearms if necessary, he won his way through and could lay claim to being the first outsider to see the forbidden city of the Western Mandingoes. He arrived back at Monrovia in March, 1869, thirteen months after starting on his journey.

Anderson's exploration of the Mandingo country was not widely publicized at the time, since it was so nearly contemporaneous with Henry M. Stanley's more spectacular achievements in the Congo, and has been almost forgotten. Nevertheless, Anderson gave the world its first knowledge of a part of Africa never before penetrated by Western man. His account of his journey—modest, clear, and concise—was considered of sufficient importance to warrant distribution by the Smithsonian Institution, with a preface written by the secretary of the Institution, Joseph Henry.[8] It is worth noting that the tribesmen of the country Anderson traversed always called him an American, and he frequently referred to himself as an American, although he was a Liberian citizen.

Seys was succeeded as Minister and Consul General by J. Milton Turner, who was the representative of the United States in Liberia until 1878. During his long term of office Turner forwarded to Washington a series of dispatches in which he reported on the state of the country and described in detail practically everything that happened. He continually urged closer commercial relations, both in the interest of the United States and its businessmen and for the improvement of Liberia itself. He gave detailed information, gained at first hand, on the soil, climate, resources, geography, and ethnology of Liberia. Late in his tour of duty he transmitted to Washington a careful and closely considered study of the coffee-growing potential of the country, urging that the cultivation of coffee in Liberia would benefit his own coffee-drinking nation and also solve Liberia's economic difficulties.[9]

Even as late as Turner's time in Liberia there were still numerous Americans who visualized Africa as a refuge for the Negroes of the

---

[8] Benjamin J. K. Anderson, *Narrative of a Journey to Musardu, the Capital of the Western Mandingoes* (New York, 1870).

It has not been possible to identify "Musardu" positively, but it seems to have been close to (or may be identical with) the city now called N'Zérékoré.

[9] *Foreign Relations, 1872–1873*, pp. 330–337, and *1879*, pp. 699–701. Turner believed that Liberian coffee was the best in the world.

United States. On February 15, 1878, Turner reported that the American bark *Liberia* had just arrived at Monrovia with fifty-three immigrants, mostly from North Carolina and Mississippi. Also among the passengers were two "commissioners of emigration," prospecting for homes for Negroes from Arkansas.[10]

Neither Turner nor any of his successors, however, seems to have found it necessary to give much time to problems arising from the migration of American Negroes to Liberia. There was probably never any great desire among very many of the Negroes to return to the land of their ancestors, and emancipation had effectively killed whatever may have existed. But other matters that claimed Turner's attention were of direct interest to the United States government in its capacity of informal sponsor and protector of Liberia. One of Turner's first dispatches must have been a disappointment and shock to Washington. On October 25, 1871, very shortly after he had presented his credentials, he reported that the administration had been overthrown by a revolution.[11]

The revolution was bloodless, but it was an indication of a problem that was to beset Liberia off and on for many years—the instability of the government because of the economic weakness of the country. Of more immediate and pressing interest was the relationship of the Liberians to the native tribes, who regarded them with dislike and suspicion as though they were white men. The tribes were bitterly resentful of all attempts by Liberian authorities to establish or exercise any control, and, unfortunately, the American-Liberians regarded the indigenous people with the not unusual contempt of a civilized man for an uncouth savage. Trouble broke out in September, 1875, when the Grebos, who numbered nearly thirty thousand, revolted and formally declared war on the Liberian government. On September 13 Turner notified Washington that the Grebos, well supplied with Snyder rifles and ammunition (of French manufacture), had attacked the settlement at Cape Palmas. Some of the Grebos were thought to have received military training at the Episcopal mission schools that had been established in their country! The attack at Cape Palmas was pressed with vigor, and it was repulsed only because

---

[10] *Foreign Relations, 1878–1879*, pp. 523–525.
[11] *Foreign Relations, 1872–1873*, p. 323.

the Liberians were able to muster the artillery that was needed.[12]

It took Turner's messages more than a month to reach Washington from Monrovia, but upon their receipt Secretary of State Hamilton Fish acted promptly. Because it was "understood that some American citizens were located there," an American warship was ordered to Cape Palmas for their protection. The arrival of the American ship enhanced the prestige of the Liberian government, and the Grebos fully understood the threat in her guns and marines. The Grebo rebellion died out, with the Liberians firmly in possession of Cape Palmas and the Grebos reluctantly acknowledging Liberian authority.[13] Nevertheless, Liberian political instability continued. In January, 1878, for example, Turner reported that the President and several members of the Cabinet had been impeached and a son of a former president had been arraigned for conspiring to assassinate certain members of the Congress. However, in spite of the intense feelings and animosities aroused, Liberian political disorders seldom became extreme. A new administration took office quietly, and the would-be assassin, on being convicted, was fined one hundred dollars.[14]

During the 1870's Liberia lay well outside the mainstream of world politics; but when the scramble for African territory by the Great Powers began in the 1880's, the little country was hurled violently into the current. France, endeavoring to regain the world position it felt it had lost in 1871, was vigorously expanding its African empire—and French territory was adjacent to Liberia.

The first indications of a movement that was to cause trouble for Liberia and diplomatic complications for the United States appeared in March, 1878, in an incident that did not immediately concern either country. In 1880, almost two years after the occurrence, Minister John H. Smyth, Turner's successor, reported that French troops had landed on the island of Matacong, about twelve miles off the mouth of the Mellacourie River. The Governor of Sierra Leone protested at once, as Great Britain claimed the island and had recently begun to collect customs duties there. But the French were actively extending their African empire in the region where Liberia lay and were even

---

[12] *Foreign Relations, 1875*, pp. 832–835.
[13] *Ibid.*, p. 836.
[14] *Foreign Relations, 1878–1879*, pp. 520–523.

willing to take the chance of offending Great Britain in realizing their colonial ambitions.[15]

A short time after this incident, Smyth was informed by the Liberian Secretary of State that France was desirous of assuming a protectorate over Liberia. "As evidence of this," the American official wrote to his government, "a dispatch was shown to me from the Liberian consul-general [M. Carrance, at Bordeaux], addressed to the secretary, in which a protectorate was proposed and urged by that officer, who indicates the advantages to accrue to Liberia from such a relation with France."[16]

Immediately upon receipt of Smyth's dispatch, the Acting Secretary of State, William Hunter, directed the American Minister in Paris to make "judicious and confidential inquiries." Minister Edward F. Noyes replied six weeks later that the French government had no desire to assume a protectorate over Liberia. The proposal had originated with Leopold Carrance himself and was probably seconded by M. Huart, the Liberian consul in Paris. Both these gentlemen had axes to grind. In fact, Huart had spent most of his time and effort in trying to persuade the Liberian government to institute a decoration for which he would be eligible.[17]

Later, Smyth reported the arrival at Monrovia of the French man-of-war *Talisman* with orders to salute the Liberian flag and carry out any mission which the President of Liberia might indicate; the gesture obviously was intended to set Liberian fears and suspicions at rest.[18] At Monrovia, Smyth remained deeply suspicious of French motives, as was obvious when he reported the details of a proposed mining concession which was being promoted by Huart in Paris—a

---

[15] *Foreign Relations, 1880,* pp. 704–705.

[16] *Foreign Relations, 1879,* p. 718. At this time Liberia, like other small countries, appointed its consular officers from among citizens of the countries where the consulates were located. Such officials were compensated by occasional consular fees and by the prestige accompanying such titles as "consul general." In 1879 the two Liberian consular officers in France, a consul general at Bordeaux and a consul in Paris, were both Frenchmen.

[17] *Foreign Relations, 1879,* pp. 341–342.

[18] Nothing has ever come to light to gainsay the conclusion that the French government was not officially involved, but it is possible that without prompt American diplomatic intervention Carrance's scheme might have developed into something serious. See John D. Hargreaves, *Prelude to the Partition of West Africa* (London, 1963), p. 294.

concession that would have granted complete control over all mines and mineral resources in Liberia for a period of fifty years. Smyth openly expressed the belief that Liberia was a most desirable annexation for any nation hunting for African possessions.[19]

Liberian affairs, and American involvement, were complicated further in the fall of 1879. The Grebos, still chafing under the authority of the American-Liberians, again broke into revolt, this time proclaiming themselves British subjects. If they hoped to bring about British intervention, their hopes were not fulfilled. Firm measures were taken by the Liberian government, supported by two American warships, and the movement soon collapsed. The Grebo chiefs complained that they were "menaced" aboard the *Essex* and were threatened by the arrival of the *Ticonderoga*—but they yielded.

The European powers, in their relations with Liberia, tacitly recognized the special position of the United States. For example, the commanding officer of the French warship *Talisman*, upon arriving at Monrovia following the flurry over a French protectorate, first called on the American Minister and requested him to arrange an audience with the President. Similarly, in December, 1879, Captain Doermann, of the Royal Netherlands Navy, sought the good offices of Minister Smyth when he brought his ship, the *Alkmaar*, to Monrovia. Smyth accompanied Doermann to his interview with the President and heartily seconded the Dutchman's suggestion on the desirability of opening additional Liberian ports to trade.[20]

In fact, the American Minister at Monrovia seems to have acquired an international position, frequently representing the United States, Liberia, and some third power simultaneously. This fact was clearly illustrated early in 1881, when a German merchant ship, the *Carlos*, struck an uncharted rock on the Kru coast and sank. The officers and crew escaped in the ship's boats but were set upon by the Krumen, beaten, and robbed. The German Minister in Washington informed Secretary of State William N. Evarts that the Imperial Government was sending the corvette *Victoria* to Liberia to assist the authorities in punishing the looters, in "the general interest of all commercial nations." The German government requested that the

---

[19] *Foreign Relations, 1880*, pp. 692–693, 705–706.
[20] *Ibid.*, pp. 693–700, 705–706.

American Minister at Monrovia be informed as to the German ship's mission and be instructed to render such assistance as might be possible.[21]

Evarts promptly sent a dispatch to Smyth, directing the assistance the German Minister had requested. It was understood, Evarts said, that the Krumen who robbed the crew of the *Carlos* were not pirates but were "wreckers," outlaws over whom the Liberian government had no effective control. In the circumstances the United States presumed that Liberia would be glad to avail itself of German assistance in making its power felt. Had the case involved an American ship and crew, the United States would have considered it entirely proper for Liberia to request such aid as Germany was now offering.

Smyth, before he received Evarts' instructions, had already acted on his own initiative. The German consul at Monrovia had formally protested to the Liberian government, which was unable to take any effective punitive measures against the tribesmen. The *Victoria* arrived at Monrovia on February 26, 1881; Commander von Valois had called immediately at the American legation to pay his respects and request the American Minister's aid, as required by his orders from Berlin.

One may infer that Smyth advised Liberian officials to comply with the German requests, although there seems to be no specific statement in any available records that he gave such advice. Liberian President A. W. Gardiner and Secretary of State Edward W. Blyden agreed at once to pay a moderate indemnity of $3,500 and to accompany Von Valois to the scene of the crime. There, after a brief investigation, the President ordered the guilty village evacuated, after which the *Victoria* shelled it. The destruction was completed by a landing party from the corvette, accompanied by a Liberian officer.[22]

Late in 1881 the *Victoria* again came to Monrovia, because Liberia had failed to pay the indemnity agreed upon. On November 10 Smyth informed Washington that Von Valois had finally sailed for the Cape Verde Islands after receiving $5,375 which the Liberian government had managed somehow to scrape together.[23]

---

[21] *Foreign Relations, 1882,* p. 734.
[22] *Ibid.,* pp. 734–736.
[23] *Foreign Relations, 1882–1883,* p. 380.

During the heyday of empire building in Africa by the great powers of Europe, Great Britain seemed to be, next to France, the main threat to Liberian territory. Unfortunately, some of the tribes in the areas bordering upon Sierra Leone were beyond the control of the Liberian government, and British traders resented any attempts by the government to enforce its laws and orders. In addition, the boundaries between Liberia and Sierra Leone were vague, both countries claiming certain areas. Thus by 1866 the expansionists of Sierra Leone were claiming regions to which Liberia had acquired rights as far back as 1852. The two interested countries agreed upon an international boundary commission, with an American, Commodore R. W. Shufeldt, as arbitrator. The first sessions of the commission were supposed to take place in the early fall of 1878, but Liberia failed to appoint commissioners in time. When the commissioners finally got together in the spring of 1879, they found themselves unable to agree. The British commissioners denied being bound by the decisions of the American arbitrator, and the commission broke up without accomplishing anything.[24]

The disputed boundary had remained unsettled for several years, when suddenly, without warning, on March 20, 1882, a flotilla of British gunboats appeared at Monrovia. Sir Arthur Havelock, Governor of Sierra Leone, who was on board the flagship, served what amounted to an ultimatum upon the helpless Liberian government: British claims to territory up to the River Maffa must be acknowledged immediately and an indemnity of £8,500 be paid to certain British traders for injuries inflicted upon them in 1871 *by tribes in the territory which Great Britain now claimed.*[25]

The United States took such diplomatic action as was possible to aid Liberia. The difficulty lay in the fact that the British expansionists were willing and ready to use force; the United States was not. President Chester A. Arthur informed Congress that through its Ministers at London and Monrovia the government had "endeavored to aid Liberia in its differences with Great Britain touching the north-

[24] *Foreign Relations, 1878–1879*, pp. 256–266, and *1879*, p. 717; Hargreaves, *Prelude to the Partition of West Africa*, p. 242.

[25] Nathaniel R. Richardson, *Liberia's Past and Present* (London, 1959), p. 110; Charles Morrow Wilson, *Liberia* (New York, 1947), pp. 17–18.

western boundary of that country," and added that the prospect of a compromise was good by which Liberia would not lose any territory.[26]

Nevertheless, Sir Arthur Havelock returned to Monrovia with his gunboats in September, demanding immediate ratification of the treaty which he had dictated earlier in the year. The Liberian Senate refused, and a few months later British troops from Sierra Leone marched into the disputed territory, which has been a part of Sierra Leone ever since. Recognizing the futility of further resistance to the British colossus, Liberia finally acknowledged British claims by a treaty signed at London on November 11, 1885.[27]

For a few years Liberia ceased to be the focus of American diplomatic interest in Africa, but in the mid 1880's the calm was sharply shattered. The French empire builders could no longer be restrained. Early in December, 1886, Smyth sent a dispatch to Washington saying that, a few days before, Lieutenant P. Aroux, of the French gunboat *Gabes*, had paid a courtesy call on the President. During the conversation the fact came out that the *Gabes* had anchored for several days at Berreiby before coming to Monrovia. But Aroux failed to mention that while at Berreiby he had negotiated a treaty with the Africans there. Berreiby, lying some distance east of Cape Palmas, was in territory that was clearly and unmistakably Liberian. Smyth had obtained his information about Aroux's activities there from the agent of the German trading firm of A. Woermann. Smyth reminded the State Department of Carrance's attempt to bring about a French protectorate over Liberia and mentioned that in 1884 a French firm had leased Kent Island, in the River Mana, without any reference to the Liberian government, dealing with the islanders as though they were an independent people. Upon representations by the United States, the French government had disallowed the lease, but with such precedents in mind Smyth was suspicious of all French activities. He urged strongly that Aroux and any treaties with which he was involved be investigated.[28]

The Secretary of State at once directed the Minister at Paris to

---

[26] *Foreign Relations, 1883*, pp. viii–ix.

[27] See Richardson, *Liberia's Past and Present*, p. 110, and Hargreaves, *Prelude to the Partition of West Africa*, p. 243.

[28] *Foreign Relations, 1886*, pp. 298–299.

question the French Foreign Office whether there was "any foundation for the report that France [had] assumed to treat with Liberian tribes as independent."[29] It became apparent not only that France was treating with the tribes as independent but that encroaching upon territory supposed to be a part of Liberia was definitely a part of French policy and ambition in that region. In July, 1886, information reached Washington that another French naval officer, Captain E. Dumont, of the *Voltigeur,* had been at Berreiby by order of his government, which had directed him to "protect" the people of that place.[30] In response to inquiries, the French Foreign Office was polite but completely unyielding, maintaining that France was undertaking no aggression against Liberia, entertained no designs upon Liberian territory, and was merely claiming what belonged to it by "the ties, already old, which unite to France the populations of Grand and Petit Beriby." The American Minister at Paris, Robert M. McLane, was shown a treaty negotiated in 1868 by a Lieutenant Crespin, of the French Navy, which, it was asserted, gave France a paramount and incontestable right to the territories it now claimed. In that treaty three of the local potentates—Mané, "King of Little Beriby," Damba-Gué, "King of Grand Beriby," and Rika, "King of Basha and Bassa-Wappoo"—had agreed to full French sovereignty over their territories and conceded to France the right to erect fortifications and build naval bases. They had further agreed never to make treaties with other countries without French permission.[31]

The diplomatic interchange between Washington and Paris continued for months. Secretary of State Thomas F. Bayard pointed out that Liberian title to the lands in question was based upon purchases made by the American Colonization Society in 1846. When Liberia became an independent state, he added, the Society had reserved ownership of every other square mile of the country for future immigrants from the United States. In other words, half the disputed territory was legally owned by United States citizens.

President Grover Cleveland, in his annual message to Congress, on December 6, 1886, remarked upon the affair:

---

[29] *Ibid.*
[30] *Ibid.*, pp. 305–307.
[31] *Ibid.*, pp. 271–272, 307.

The weakness of Liberia and the difficulty of maintaining effective sovereignty over its outlying districts, have exposed that republic to encroachment. It cannot be forgotten that this distant community is an offshoot of our own system, owing its origin to the associated benevolence of American citizens. . . . Although a formal protectorate over Liberia is contrary to our traditional policy, the moral right and duty of the United States to assist in all proper ways the maintenance of its integrity is obvious, and has been consistently announced during nearly half a century.[32]

Unhappily for Liberia, the significant word in President Cleveland's remarks was *distant*. The American people could not become passionately interested in the fate of a small country on the other side of the world. The United States, moreover, for all its impressive size and population, was militarily a second-rate state. France, on the other hand, was one of the foremost military and naval powers of the world and was energetically extending its dominions in every direction.

In these circumstances the only recourse for Liberia and the United States was continued diplomatic correspondence and interchange. Many Americans, possibly even those in high office, believed optimistically that reason, right, and argument would prevail over selfish national interests. Late in 1887 the Liberian Secretary of State wrote to Bayard, saying that Carrance—still representing Liberia in his own country—believed that he must be granted special powers to handle the negotiations, as the French Foreign Ministry had refused to treat with the American Minister on the matter. Secretary Bayard's reply was that the American Minister was acting as a disinterested conciliator, not as a Liberian representative.[33]

The situation was complicated by a rebellion among the tribes of part of the territory that was in dispute, during which a party of American missionaries was plundered and otherwise abused. The President of Liberia begged for active American assistance, or intervention, maintaining that under existing treaties such action was called for. Bayard, somewhat legalistically, denied the right of Liberia to demand American military help; such a demand, he said, must come from the injured American citizens—and none of the mission-

[32] *Ibid.*, p. vii.
[33] *Foreign Relations, 1888,* pp. 1084–1086.

aries involved in the incident had presented any such request.[34]

Meanwhile, French appetite for African territory was unsatisfied. The dispute was still going on when French emissaries made a treaty with a Moslem ruler known as Almamy Samadu (better known now as Samori ibn Lafiya Ture), with whom Liberia had concluded treaties several years earlier. He asserted that his treaties with the French were commercial treaties only, but the French maintained that he had agreed to French protection, and French troops, to enforce the claim, immediately occupied his country in the eastern part of Liberia.[35]

In London the American Minister, Robert Todd Lincoln, son of the Emancipator, discussed this new development with the Liberian Minister, Edward W. Blyden, and on August 14, 1892, had an interview with Lord Salisbury, the Prime Minister. Salisbury was noncommittal, referring Lincoln to a parliamentary paper (Africa No. 7, 1892), in which he had directed the British Ambassador at Paris to notify the French government that British acknowledgment of French treaties on the Ivory Coast was not to be taken as prejudicing Liberian claims. Further than that, Salisbury declined to go.[36]

Since France, in its imperial enthusiasm, would yield to no argument but the sword, and since the United States would not, and could not, resort to force, Liberia was defeated. Prior to the incidents recounted in the preceding paragraphs, a treaty had been drawn up whereby the boundary between Liberia and French territory was placed at the Cavalla River. The Liberian government signed in December, 1892, formally ceding to France an area which Liberia had actually occupied almost from its inception as a state.

The dispute with France was the last major diplomatic episode involving the United States in Liberian affairs in the nineteenth century. Liberian territory was encroached upon by both France and Great Britain. Yet it is probable that without American diplomatic support Liberia would have vanished from the map during the race of the major powers to divide African territory.

---

[34] *Ibid.*, pp. 1081–1083.
[35] *Foreign Relations, 1892*, pp. 231–232.
[36] *Ibid.*

Chapter 3

Bula Matari and the Congo

In Africa, Liberian affairs constituted the main diplomatic concern of the United States government during the period between the Civil War and the end of the century. Americans collectively had little interest in matters outside their own country, and the United States took no part in the scramble for African territory in the 1870's and 1880's. But that is not to say that individual Americans were indifferent to developments in the Dark Continent. American merchants continued to trade with Africa; American prospectors, engineers, and technicians played major roles in opening up the mineral resources of the continent; American missionaries were in the van of the effort to bring the Gospel to Africans; and American explorers and adventurers were among the foremost in solving the geographical and ethnological puzzles of the interior.

The name which stands out in the annals of African exploration is that of Henry Morton Stanley. Late in life Stanley resumed British citizenship and accepted a knighthood, but at the time of his explorations in Africa he regarded himself as an American, and his efforts were largely financed by Americans.

Born John Rowlands, at Denbigh, Wales, on June 10, 1841, he was abandoned by his family and placed in the St. Asaph Union Workhouse. He remained in the orphanage until 1856, when, furious at the brutal tyranny, he thrashed the headmaster and ran away. After numerous misadventures, he shipped as a cabin boy for New Orleans, where he was befriended in 1859 by a local merchant. When the Civil War broke out, Stanley (who had assumed his benefactor's name) enlisted in the Confederate Army. Taken prisoner at the Battle of Shiloh, he was released, after a brief captivity, to enlist in the Union Army. Ill-health, however, caused his early discharge from the army.

He wandered from place to place for a time, finally enlisting in the Union Navy.

While in the navy Stanley supplemented his pay by acting as an unofficial correspondent for the New York papers, and after the war he joined the staff of the New York *Herald*. He soon became a star reporter, covering a wide field, from Indian campaigns in the Far West to the British expedition to Abyssinia in 1867. In 1869 he was in Spain, writing on a civil war in that country, when he received a telegram directing him to report to James Gordon Bennett, the owner of the *Herald*, in Paris.

Bennett's instructions were broad. Stanley was to find Dr. Livingstone, the famous missionary-explorer, who had vanished into Central Africa several years earlier, in 1866, and had not been heard from since. Stanley was given a free hand and a "blank check" for expenses.

Arriving at Zanzibar on an American whaler in January, 1871, Stanley noted that the greater part of the vessels in port were American, principally from New York and Salem. Describing their cargoes, he wrote: "They arrive loaded with American sheeting, brandy, gunpowder, muskets, beads, English cottons, brass-wire, china-ware, and other notions, and depart with ivory, gum-copal, cloves, hides, cowries, sesamum, pepper, and cocoa-nut oil."[1]

After weeks of preparation at Zanzibar, Stanley loaded his supplies and equipment, his soldiers and porters, onto four Arab dhows and sailed for Bagamoyo on the mainland. In his preparations he had been helped by the American consul, and his equipment included two boats purchased from Americans in Zanzibar. On board one of the dhows was a fine horse presented to him by a merchant from Salem who had lived in Zanzibar for many years. As the dhows moved out from the port, Stanley hoisted to the masthead an American flag which had been presented by the consul's wife.[2]

With the American flag carried at the head of the column, Stanley led this large and well-equipped expedition and made his way across Tanganyika to Ujiji, several times fighting hostile Africans. At Ujiji

---

[1] Henry M. Stanley, *How I Found Livingstone: Travels, Adventures, and Discoveries in Central Africa, Including Four Months' Residence with Dr. Livingstone* (London, 1873), pp. 2–5, 11.

[2] *Ibid.*, pp. 31, 39–40.

he found Dr. Livingstone and supplied him with food and medicines. Together they explored Lake Tanganyika and went westward to the Lualaba River, which Livingstone was convinced was the upper Nile.

Livingstone, still fired with his mission to find the source of the Nile, refused to leave Africa. Stanley returned to England and found himself famous. At first, certain professional explorers and so-called experts on Africa refused to believe that he had found Livingstone, declared that the geographical information he published was impossible, and accused him of being a fraud. But such charges were soon stilled by incontrovertible evidence that he was telling the truth.

Possibly some of the opposition to recognition of Stanley's achievements, and a degree of prejudice against Stanley himself, came from the fact that he was regarded as an American. There is no doubt that the unfavorable reception which he initially received from some Englishmen served to accentuate his American mannerisms and his American accent.[3]

Stanley's brief contact with Africa and with David Livingstone transformed his life. Thenceforth his mission was the opening of the Dark Continent. In 1873 he accompanied Lord Wolseley's expedition to Ashanti as a war correspondent and attracted the attention of the commander in chief by his coolness under fire. The short, smoothly conducted Ashanti campaign contributed to Stanley's preparation for his future work by giving him further insight into African psychology and customs and by affording him the opportunity to observe and study Wolseley's meticulously careful plans and arrangements.

While en route to England, after the close of the campaign, Stanley learned that Livingstone had died months before, alone in the African wilderness. The body of the great explorer, medical man, and humanitarian arrived in England on April 15, 1874, and three

---

[3] Several years later he replied to the question, "Are you an American citizen?": "I am undoubtedly a citizen of the United States. I travel under an American passport and always have. I claim and possess all rights of an American citizen. . . . I always have with me the emblem of nationality—in civilized countries the passport—in savage countries the flag of the United States of America, and I have never sought the protection, aid, or counsel of any foreign agent, resident, minister or consul. . . . I have sacrificed honours and distinctions for having done deeds worthy of honour because I am an American citizen."

The response is quoted in Frank Hird, *H. M. Stanley: The Authorized Life* (London, 1935), p. 202.

days later was buried in Westminster Abbey. Stanley was one of the pallbearers.

No one can say whether Stanley took advantage of the public interest in Africa aroused by Livingstone's funeral to promote a plan which he must have formulated long before. A few days after the funeral, however, he suggested to Edward Levy-Lawson, the owner and manager of the London *Daily Telegraph*, that a new expedition to Africa be organized to complete the explorations which Livingstone had not lived to finish and to unravel the African mysteries which Livingstone's death left unsolved.

After a very brief discussion, Levy-Lawson agreed tentatively, and a cablegram inviting James Gordon Bennett's participation was sent off. The reply was simple and to the point: "Yes. Bennett."[4] And so was conceived in 1874 the "Anglo-American Expedition for the Discovery of the Nile and Congo Sources." Following approximately his old route, from Zanzibar Stanley plunged again into Africa and vanished from the ken of the world for almost three years. Nine hundred and ninety-nine days later he emerged from the forest near the mouth of the Congo; he himself was the sole white survivor, and more than half the Zanzibaris who formed the party had died or had been killed in fights with savage tribesmen along the river.

Stanley had crossed the continent from east to west, accomplishing more than any other previous exploring expedition. Geographically, he had resolved many of the hitherto unanswered problems of Africa. He not only had measured the length and shore line of Lake Tanganyika but also had determined the size of Lake Victoria and proved that it was a single lake. He had discovered a previously unknown body of water, Lake Mweru, and had traversed the hitherto unknown course of the mighty Congo. Politically, his letters from Uganda urging that missionaries be sent to the court of M'Tesa (Mutesa) extended British interests into the interior of East Africa and led ultimately to the establishment of the Uganda Protectorate. Commercially, Stanley's expedition opened up vast regions of Central and East Africa to European and American merchants. Leopold II,

---

[4] Henry M. Stanley, *Through the Dark Continent; or, The Sources of the Nile, around the Great Lakes of Equatorial Africa, and down the Livingstone River to the Atlantic Ocean* (New York, 1878), II, 2–3.

King of the Belgians, hoped to gain wealth from the Congo; Sir William Mackinnon and his associates of the Imperial East Africa Company looked for profits in Kenya and Uganda.

Stanley's reappearance, after he had been given up as lost by most of the world, electrified Europe and America. In the months following his return to Europe, statesmen and scholars vied in heaping honors on him. The King of Italy sent a portrait of himself with a complimentary inscription; the principal geographical societies tendered him their gold medals; Queen Victoria received Stanley in audience and presented him with a diamond-studded gold snuffbox. The explorer was especially proud of a vote of thanks passed unanimously by both houses of the Congress of his adopted country.[5]

Queen Victoria and the King of Italy were not the only royal personages interested in the man who had braved the Congo. Reigning in Brussels was King Leopold II, a wily and capable diplomat and the most astute businessman among the crowned heads of the world. For some time Leopold had been interested in various projects in the tropics, including Africa, but in the competition for African territory he was handicapped by the fact that his country was not a great power. Nor did Belgium have any time-honored claims or position in Africa that could be used for bargaining or for further extension of influence. On September 12, 1876, while Stanley was still in the Congo, Leopold had convened a distinguished gathering of geographers and travelers at the royal palace in Brussels. In addition to the Belgians, there were delegates from Great Britain, Germany, France, Austria-Hungary, Russia, and Italy. There were no American delegates, but almost at the King's right hand stood Henry Shelton Sanford, who in the 1860's had been the United States Minister to Belgium for eight years.

Leopold opened the conference with a graceful speech of welcome in which he expressed the hope that the meeting would result in the forming of an international organization with a definite plan for the final suppression of the slave trade and for the opening of Africa to civilization. Three days later the conference adjourned, having laid the foundation for the establishment of the "International

---

[5] Byron Farwell, *The Man Who Presumed: A Biography of Henry M. Stanley* (New York, 1957), pp. 169–170.

Association for the Exploration and Civilization of Central Africa," of which King Leopold was President, to be administered by an executive committee. The committee consisted of three members, one for each of the three principal language groups of the Western world—English, Germanic, and Latin. The British government, however, was reluctant to become involved, even though the Association was supposedly an unofficial organization. The British member, Sir Bartle Frere, was soon appointed Governor of the Cape of Good Hope, and Great Britain withdrew. Frere was replaced at once by Henry Shelton Sanford, who thereafter represented all English-speaking peoples in the affairs of the Association.[6]

The Anglo-American Expedition had established Stanley as one of the world's greatest explorers and as the greatest living authority on Africa. Despite the fact that a few still regarded him as primarily a notoriety-seeking poseur, his reputation was firmly founded, both in popular estimate and in scientific circles, even before he returned to Europe from the Congo. King Leopold and the executive committee of the newly formed International Association decided immediately that Stanley was the man for their purposes—to undertake and execute their African projects. On his arrival at Marseilles early in 1878, Sanford and another member of the committee were on hand to meet him and sound him out. Stanley listened to what they had to

---

[6] Henry M. Stanley, *The Congo and the Founding of Its Free State: A Story of Work and Exploration* (New York, 1885), II, 33–38; Henry Wellington Wack, *The Story of the Congo Free State: Social, Political, and Economic Aspects of the Belgian System of Government in Central Africa* (New York and London, 1905), pp. 8–13.

Sanford is usually referred to as "General" Sanford, and one writer has described him as "a grizzled American soldier." He was not, however, a soldier at all but a career diplomat in days when American diplomatic appointments were usually awarded as prizes in the spoils system. He had held diplomatic posts at St. Petersburg, Frankfurt, and Paris before becoming the United States Minister to Belgium in 1861. In Brussels he was active in watching and thwarting Confederate efforts in Europe. He also assisted the state of Minnesota in obtaining cannon in Europe to arm its artillery for the Civil War, and for this he was made a major general in the Minnesota militia—hence the title "General." Sanford represented the United States at international conferences at Berlin in 1885 and at Brussels in 1890. Late in life he was the founder and promoter of the city of Sanford, Florida, where his papers are preserved in the Sanford Memorial Library. (This sketch is based on the account of his life in the *Dictionary of American Biography*.)

47

say. He was interested, but at the time he had had his fill of exploring. He was willing to give the International Association the benefit of his experience, but, he told Sanford, he would not then consider returning to Africa.[7]

There was an aspect of Stanley's character which is usually overlooked by historians but which, added to his prestige and his knowledge of the inner recesses of the Congo, made him a logical choice to execute Leopold's plans. Stanley was a man who combined steel-like resolution and hardness with a military loyalty toward those for whom he was then working. His early unhappy experiences in an orphanage, rejection by his own family, Civil War service, years as a star reporter for the dictatorial Bennett, an innate firmness of will —all these probably produced his ability to drive both subordinates and himself as ruthlessly and remorselessly as any Napoleon or Genghis Khan. Some of Stanley's contemporaries recognized this. His African name was Bula Matari—the "Breaker of Stones." An elderly African who had known him said to Emory Ross, "Mr. Stanley, he was a har-rd man!" And no less a person than Queen Victoria, after her audience with him, characterized him as "determined."[8]

A man of softer nature than Stanley could never have overcome the obstacles or surmounted the discouragements encountered in the epic voyage from the headwaters of the Congo to its mouth. Such a person is often an unpleasant associate but, given something to do, will accomplish his mission without thought of comfort, safety, or even humanity: men are merely implements with which to force his way to the assigned goal. The virtues of Stanley were those of the hard-driving American frontiersmen and businessmen—and many of the Americans who went to Africa seemed cast in the same mold.

Leopold and his committee were patient—and persevering. By August of the next year Stanley had recovered his health and spirits, and a life of relative idleness was beginning to pall. He was rebuffed in Great Britain; in spite of the honors that had been given him there he was unable to persuade anyone in the kingdom to take more than an academic interest in the Congo. A letter from one of

[7] Stanley, *The Congo and the Founding of Its Free State,* I, 21.
[8] Emory Ross, *Out of Africa* (New York, 1936), p. 8; Farwell, *The Man Who Presumed,* pp. 85–86.

the committeemen, suggesting a meeting at Paris, found him in a much more receptive mood than he had been at Marseilles. An urgent invitation from Leopold to come to the palace at Brussels on a certain date found Stanley willing to consider whatever might be proposed. On his arrival he was surrounded by a group of financiers, explorers, geographers, and philanthropists from several countries. All these gentlemen evinced a deep interest in Africa, and for a whole day they plied him with questions.

Some of their questions Stanley could answer offhand; others were unanswerable. But before the meeting broke up, it was resolved that a new organization should be formed, the "Comité d'Etudes du Haut Congo." An initial fund of £20,000 was subscribed for immediate use, and every subscriber bound himself to donate more if necessary. It was further decided that an expedition should be sent to Africa as soon as possible to obtain accurate information on doubtful points and to establish stations to serve as bases for later activities. By unanimous vote, Stanley was invited to take command of the expedition and act as representative of the Comité.

Thus, Henry M. Stanley became the mainstay of Leopold's plans in Africa, the driving force that made their fulfillment possible. Without his services, the vast Congo basin would probably have been taken over by one or another of the Great Powers, and the course of Central African history would have been far different. Stanley, believing thoroughly in the benevolence and disinterestedness of Leopold's purposes and the value to Africa and Western civilization of the Comité's projects, supported and fostered both with unswerving loyalty.[9]

Stanley's activities during the next few years constituted the beginnings of the Congo Free State with King Leopold as its sovereign and the inception of European penetration into the still unknown regions of the Congo. Stanley set to work with his usual energy, purchasing equipment, interviewing applicants, and engaging suitable men. His task, the organizing of settlements intended as permanent bases, required that he foresee and provide for any and all contin-

---

[9] Although the Comité d'Etudes du Haut Congo was nominally separate and distinct from the International Association, in a short time it became, for all practical purposes, no more than an extension of the Association.

49

gencies. Enormous amounts of equipment and supplies were needed; the numbers of men whose employment was anticipated and the extent and complexity of the expected operations necessitated both an elaborate organization and a grasp of details not to be expected of persons without practical experience in the tropical forest. By unremitting labor Stanley was able to arrive at the mouth of the Congo within a few months, ready to start on his mission.

Unlike his two previous expeditions into the wilds of Africa, this venture was neither American nor Anglo-American; it was international. But the United States was still a factor: in addition to Sanford in Belgium, the International Association included an American committee in New York City, presided over by John H. B. Latrobe, who was also the president of the still-active American Colonization Society and one of the founders of Liberia.[10] Stanley's immediate staff of assistants included an American named Sparhawk, an old "Africa hand" upon whom he came to rely heavily.

For most of the next five years Stanley lived in Africa, extending his explorations, establishing and supervising stations, surveying and building roads, and, most important of all, negotiating treaties with numerous African dignitaries and potentates whereby they placed themselves under the protection of the Association. This part of Stanley's mission was not publicized—a circumstance which tended to cast an air of mystery about the expedition and led to the groundless suspicion in some quarters that Stanley, an American citizen, was laying the foundations for an American empire in Africa.[11] Some recent writers have felt that there was something discreditable about Stanley's treaty-making activities, although the major European powers were doing exactly the same thing.

Stanley's contemporaries did not then regard the Association as a mere front for Leopold's private design; few doubted that its primary motives were other than philanthropic, humanitarian, and scientific.

---

[10] Jesse Siddall Reeves, *The International Beginnings of the Congo Free State* (Johns Hopkins University Studies in Historical and Political Science, Ser. 12, XI–XII; Baltimore, 1894), p. 18.

[11] Count Savorgnan de Brazza, the French explorer and empire builder, seems to have entertained this suspicion. See Albert Maurice (ed.), *H. M. Stanley: Unpublished Letters* (New York, 1957), p. 149.

Its commercial motives were open and apparent, and no one at that time looked upon such incentives as discreditable. On the contrary, these seemed only praiseworthy; the public assumed that the development of the commercial possibilities of the Congo would tend automatically toward civilizing and improving the condition of the native people.

While Stanley was establishing stations and obtaining concessions and treaties from local kings and tribal chiefs, the resurrection of ancient and almost forgotten claims to Congo territories suddenly threatened to disrupt everything the Association was trying to do. By reason of the discoveries of the early Portuguese explorers, Portugal had always maintained a shadowy claim to the Congo, but none of the European powers paid much attention to Portuguese assertions. In the mid-nineteenth century a rather feeble Portuguese effort to establish authority on the Congo had been firmly vetoed by Great Britain, because traders of several nations were already installed there and because the slave trade flourished under the Portuguese flag. Moreover, Great Britain had somewhat nebulous claims to Congo soil owing to treaties negotiated with several chiefs during British operations against the slave trade. Even so, the vast territory which Stanley had explored, and in which he was working on behalf of the Association, was still not held under international law by any "civilized" power.

Two sets of circumstances suddenly rendered the Congo important. First, Stanley's explorations suggested that the Congo basin was a region of great potential wealth and could be made accessible, and, second, the announcement of De Brazza's explorations and annexations for France, adjacent to the Congo, caused immediate alarm in London and Lisbon. French colonial policy was exclusive. If the French established themselves firmly, then the merchants, missionaries, and traders of all other nations would be shut out.

British fears of French designs resulted in the Anglo-Portuguese treaty of February 26, 1884, concluded after a long, complicated series of confidential negotiations. In its broad provisions the treaty recognized Portuguese territorial claims and provided for a joint Anglo-Portuguese commission to control navigation and traffic on the Congo River. While the treaty assured freedom of navigation on the Congo and its tributaries to shipping of all nations, the two powers had disposed of the matter as though only they were concerned. Other nations whose traders were already in the region were completely ignored, and the establishments formed by Stanley for the Association went unmentioned, as though they were not in existence.[12]

As soon as the treaty was made public, there was a wave of protest. In March, 1884, the French government announced that France would neither recognize the treaty nor consider itself bound by it. On April 18 a similar announcement was made by the German government. And in addition to objections voiced by other countries of Europe, the treaty did not meet with unanimous approval in Great Britain. British businessmen with existing interests in the Congo were distinctly displeased at the prospect of subjecting themselves to the inefficiency, maladministration, and corruption which they regarded as almost synonymous with Portuguese colonial government. Humanitarians were aghast at the idea of putting additional Africans under the power of a nation that still winked at the slave trade; Protestant missionary bodies were indignant at the possibility that Protestant missions might be handicapped or thwarted by a staunchly Roman Catholic government. Not even the strongest proponents of the treaty could deny that neither governments nor private parties with interests in the Congo had been consulted.[13]

At this time the legal status of the International Association in Africa was extremely vague. Its position was somewhat analogous to

---

[12] Roger Anstey, *Britain and the Congo in the Nineteenth Century* (Oxford, 1962), pp. 112–167; Sybil E. Crowe, *The Berlin West African Conference, 1884–1885* (London, New York, and Toronto, 1942), pp. 11–22; H. R. Fox Bourne, *Civilization in Congoland: A Story of International Wrong-Doing* (London, 1903), pp. 158–159.

Most of the writers who have discussed the Anglo-Portuguese treaty and the resulting Berlin Conference seem to be intent upon proving that Great Britain was motivated solely by philanthropic and humanitarian purposes. Fox Bourne, for example, says that Great Britain insisted upon recognizing the interests acquired by the Association and the trading rights of all nations and that the treaty was "subject to its being approved by the other Powers." Nothing in the text of the treaty indicates any such reservations. Sybil Crowe's work is so biased that her statements and conclusions can be accepted only in part and with modifications.

[13] Anstey, *Britain and the Congo in the Nineteenth Century*, pp. 113–138; Demetrius C. de K. Boulger, *The Reign of Leopold II, King of the Belgians and Founder of the Congo State, 1865–1909* (London, 1925), I, 146.

that of the American Colonization Society in early Liberia—it was exercising sovereignty without any legal or technical right to do so. It was a corporation—a private individual—in competition with recognized sovereign powers. As Stanley said in a letter to an unidentified friend, "De Brazza with his walking stick, a French flag and a few words in the presence of the whites at Leopoldville, is really stronger than Stanley with his Krupps and all material of war, faithful adherents, aid of natives, etc."[14]

With an eye to potential American commercial interests of the future, President Chester A. Arthur in his annual message to Congress, on December 4, 1883, gave the first inkling of American official interest in the Congo:

> The rich and populous valley of the Congo is being opened to commerce by a society called the International African Association, of which the King of the Belgians is the president, and a citizen of the United States [Stanley] is the chief executive officer. Large tracts of territory have been ceded to the association by native chiefs, roads have been opened, steamboats placed on the river, and the nuclei of states established at twenty-two stations under one flag which offers freedom to commerce and prohibits the slave trade. The objects of the society are philanthropic. It does not aim at permanent political control but seeks the neutrality of the valley. The United States cannot be indifferent to this work nor to the interests of their citizens involved in it. It may become advisable for us to cooperate with other commercial powers in promoting the right of trade and residence in the Congo Valley free from the interference or political control of any one nation.[15]

It is not surprising that the United States promptly recognized the sovereign rights of the International Association: there was not only a genuine American interest in the possibilities of the Congo, stimulated by national pride in the fact that an American, Henry M. Stanley, was a key figure in efforts to open the Congo, but also a suspicion that Great Britain, widely believed by Americans to be a notoriously predatory power, was seeking, unjustly, to pre-empt the Congo.

The Association's position was suddenly clarified and strengthened

---

[14] Quoted in Anstey, *Britain and the Congo in the Nineteenth Century,* p. 169.

[15] *Foreign Relations, 1883,* p. ix.

on April 22, 1884, while the controversy over the Anglo-Portuguese treaty was in full sway, by a formal American pronouncement:

> Frederick T. Frelinghuysen, Secretary of State, duly empowered therefor by the President of the United States of America, and pursuant to the advice and consent of the Senate heretofore given ... declares that ... the Government of the United States will order the officers of the United States, both on land and sea, to recognize the flag of the International Association as the flag of a friendly Government.[16]

Recognition of the Association's sovereign status was followed within a few days by French recognition and on November 8 by that of Germany. In due course the other powers followed suit, the Association took its place among the recognized governments of the world, and King Leopold of Belgium reigned over a vast African region as well.

The recognition of the Association by the United States, coming at such an opportune time, was the result of careful and skillful planning. In November, 1883, months before the Anglo-Portuguese treaty was signed, Sanford returned to the United States from Europe for the express purpose of persuading the government to recognize the Association. He was openly, frankly, and unashamedly a lobbyist— a term which had not then been invented but covers activities that in the 1880's were not regarded as in any way reprehensible or questionable. He entertained senators and representatives; he furnished information regarding the Congo to the State Department; he became acquainted with members of the Senate Committee on Foreign Relations; and everywhere he stressed the philanthropic and humanitarian purposes motivating Leopold and the Association members.[17]

---

[16] Congress, Senate, *Report of the Secretary of State Relative to Affairs of the Independent State of the Congo,* 49th Cong., 1st sess., S. Exec. Doc. 196 (1886), p. 348.

[17] See letter, W. P. Tisdale to Secretary of State Bayard, *ibid.,* pp. 379–387. Tisdale, who was the first American commercial agent accredited to the Congo Free State, thoroughly disliked Sanford and denounced him in strong terms but nevertheless accorded him grudging admiration for the skill with which he conducted negotiations. Although Sanford stimulated interest in the Congo, he would undoubtedly have failed but for American pride in the *American* explorer, Henry M. Stanley, and hopes for commercial and business opportunities in the newly opened country.

CHAPTER 4

Neutrality and Philanthropy

Confronted by the fact that the International Association was established in the Congo and recognized as sovereign there by several powers and faced with the almost unanimous opposition of all Europe, Great Britain and Portugal had no choice but to abandon the attempt to treat the Congo as a private matter between themselves. Consequently, when German Chancellor Bismarck in early October of 1884, after consultation with France, invited the United States and other interested powers to send representatives to Berlin to consider (among other items) the question of "freedom of commerce in the basin and the mouths of the Congo," the Congo was positively placed within the scope of international interest.[1]

Since the United States traditionally remained aloof from the politics of the Old World, the government had at first some hesitancy in accepting Bismarck's invitation. With the understanding that the conference was purely for discussion and the establishment of general principles and that the United States could reserve the right to decline to accept conclusions reached, the government at Washington decided to participate.

The representative designated was John A. Kasson, the American Minister at Berlin. Kasson was no novice in international diplomacy and politics. He had served several terms as a member of Congress, as well as in the legislature of his state. Under President Lincoln's administration he was an Assistant Postmaster General and was the

---

[1] Congress, Senate, *Report of the Secretary of State Relative to Affairs of the Independent State of the Congo*, 49th Cong., 1st sess., S. Exec. Doc. 196 (1886), p. 7. To infer or assume, as some writers have done, that Bismarck was merely a cat's-paw for Leopold or that the conference was summoned as a result of Machiavellian diabolatries exercised by Henry Shelton Sanford is to ascribe to Bismarck a weakness that has never been detected, even by his enemies. For reasons of his own, Bismarck saw advantages for Germany in such a conference.

United States representative at the International Postal Congress at Paris in 1863. In 1867 he was a commissioner to negotiate postal conventions with Great Britain, France, Belgium, Germany, Switzerland, and Italy. From 1877 to 1881 he was United States Minister at the court of Vienna, and at the time of Bismarck's invitation he had recently been promoted to the more critical and important diplomatic post of Minister to the German Empire.[2] On October 20, 1884, Kasson, who had already been informed that he would be the United States representative, was told by the German Foreign Office that the conference probably would hear experts on Africa. The world's foremost expert on Africa was an American citizen—Henry M. Stanley. On the same day Kasson wrote to Stanley: "Can you hold yourself at liberty to be present at Berlin a week before the meeting of the Conference on West African affairs, and during its deliberations?" Kasson was well aware that Stanley was concerned with the International Association, and in view of his government's attitude toward the Association, he saw no possible objection to having Stanley as his expert adviser. In fact, Kasson welcomed the opportunity for Stanley to present the Association's case before the conference. "This action will be in harmony with the interests which you represent," he told Stanley in his invitation. Three days later, having learned from the German Foreign Office that each delegate would be allowed an associate to sit with him, Kasson at once thought of Sanford—an experienced diplomat who was familiar with the matters to be considered and an officer of the Association. On October 23, 1884, he sent a cablegram to Washington, asking "that the usefulness of Mr. Sanford, as such an associate, be taken into consideration." Secretary of State Frelinghuysen replied the same day, fully authorizing Kasson to use Sanford, at his own discretion, provided that no additional expense to the United States government was incurred.[3]

---

[2] *Congressional Directory* (1884), 48th Cong., 1st sess., pp. 27–28. Kasson's record proves that there is little justification for Sybil Crowe's statement that he was "distinguished more by verbosity than by brains" or for the idea that he was merely a puppet in the hands of Sanford. See Sybil E. Crowe, *The Berlin West African Conference, 1884–1885* (London, New York, and Toronto, 1942), p. 97. See also Edward Younger, *John A. Kasson: Politics and Diplomacy from Lincoln to McKinley* (Iowa City, Iowa, 1955), pp. 141–152, 210–228, 278–295, 322–343.

[3] Congress, Senate, *Report of the Secretary of State Relative to Affairs of the Independent State of the Congo*, pp. 16–17.

An additional American official—W. P. Tisdale, who had been appointed as the government's commercial agent in the Congo state—was hurried to Berlin to observe the conference's proceedings. Tisdale was not formally accredited as an associate delegate, but "at the same time his position as the first and only representative sent by any Government to the State of the Congo" was to be borne in mind.[4]

On November 15, 1884, the delegates assembled for the first session. Prince Bismarck, as host, accepted the chairmanship and suggested the agenda for the conference's consideration. On the second day Kasson made a brief speech, citing the reasons for American participation and the bases of American policy and attitudes. He stressed the fact that vast regions in Central Africa had been first explored by an American citizen and that the International Association, which had established a *de facto* government in the region, included Americans in its membership, adding that "the blacks will learn from it [the Association] that the civilization and the dominion of the white man means for them peace and freedom and the development of useful commerce, free to all the world."[5]

Kasson, from his position of neutrality and international impartiality, was able to exercise a strong influence on the conference, and because he was aided and advised by Stanley and Sanford, his words carried weight. Early in the conference it became clear that many of the distinguished delegates had extremely vague ideas on African geography. Kasson suggested that Mr. Stanley enlighten them.

> He went to a chart suspended in the room, and immediately engrossed the interest of every delegate, by a vivid description of the features of the Congo basin; and finally of the [adjacent] country necessary to go with it under the same *régime* to secure the utmost freedom of communication with the two oceans.[6]

---

[1] *Ibid.*, pp. 19–20. Many—possibly all—of the charges and allegations as to deception, double dealing, and general villainy on the part of Sanford and Stanley seem to have originated with Tisdale. There was an obvious clash of personalities from the start, especially since Tisdale, who maintained that he knew as much about Africa as Stanley did, disagreed with Stanley's conclusions on the economic potential of the Congo. All of this, however, did not come out until much later, for Tisdale left Berlin without attending any of the sessions of the conference. (See *ibid.*, pp. 21, 346–387.)

[5] *Ibid.*, p. 34.

[6] *Ibid.*, p. 42.

Thus, Kasson was able to persuade the conference to adopt his suggestions on the definition to be given to the *Congo basin,* and he steadily used his influence toward the adoption of free trade with, and within, the areas defined. In other particulars, too, Kasson was active, and the final general act, or Convention, of the Berlin Conference bears the distinct imprint not only of Sanford, Stanley, and King Leopold but of the representative of the United States, Kasson.

The United States government never ratified, and hence was never formally bound by, the results of the Berlin Conference. Nevertheless, the American representative signed the Convention, and the United States government was morally a subscriber to the principles finally agreed upon.

Although Stanley's exploratory and colonizing work in the Congo had been ended before the Berlin Conference, he was not yet through with Africa. He went to the Congo a fourth time in 1887 to lead a long and arduous expedition to rescue Emin Pasha (Eduard Schnitzer), a German in Egyptian service who was isolated in Equatorial Africa by the Mahdist uprising in the Egyptian Sudan. On the outward journey, after rescuing Emin, Stanley discovered the great Ruwenzori Range (the legendary Mountains of the Moon), the Albert Edward Nyanza (Lake), and the great southwestern gulf of Lake Victoria, which had not been noted previously. He returned to England and in 1892 resumed British citizenship. He was knighted and in 1895 was elected to Parliament.[7]

The Berlin Conference marked a new departure in American diplomacy. For the first time, United States representatives had sat in a multilateral international conference considering issues and territories outside the Western Hemisphere. Despite the clear reservations under which the United States took part, people were not lacking who "viewed with alarm" what they regarded as a radical deviation from the traditions of a century and from the almost sacred precepts established by the Founding Fathers. Led by Congressman Perry Belmont, the isolationist "die-hards" attacked at once. On January 5, 1885, Belmont introduced a resolution demanding that the President

---

[7] Stanley died in London in 1904. He wanted to be buried in Westminster Abbey, next to Livingstone, but the Dean of the Abbey refused—Stanley's achievements, the Dean felt, did not warrant such national recognition.

inform Congress just why the United States was participating, and shortly before the inauguration of the new President, Grover Cleveland, he sponsored a resolution that went further:

> The House of Representatives, heedful of the admonitions of Washington, and faithful to that neutral policy of separation and peace which our situation and the wisdom of a free people have hitherto enabled us to maintain, hereby explicitly declares its dissent from the act of the President of the United States in accepting the invitation of Germany and France to participate in the International Conference at Berlin.[8]

Opponents of President Arthur's action in accepting the invitation refused to regard the disposition of the Congo as a matter of concern for the whole civilized world: Belmont, for example, stoutly maintained to the end of his life that this was purely a European problem, with which the United States had no concern. In addition, there was an absurd fear that international agreements as to navigation on the Congo might somehow be twisted into a precedent for international control over the Mississippi.[9]

Belmont, being a Democrat, easily gained the ear of President-elect Cleveland, who was inclined to be suspicious of anything suggesting international entanglement. In his annual message to Congress, Cleveland stated that, since acceptance of the Berlin Convention would have made the United States a party to an alliance, he had withdrawn the treaty and expressly refrained from asking the Senate to ratify it. Somewhat ambiguously, he added that despite the reservations under which the United States participated, the American delegates had signed the Convention just as had the plenipotentiaries of the other powers.[10]

---

[8] Quoted in his *An American Democrat: The Recollections of Perry Belmont* (2d ed.; New York, 1941), p. 314.

[9] *Ibid.*, p. 329.

[10] *Foreign Relations, 1886*, pp. viii–ix. This remark was interpreted by Kasson as an unwarranted and unnecessary reprimand. He replied in a lengthy article in the *North American Review* for February, 1886, in which he refuted, point by point, all the arguments which had been adduced by Belmont and other traditionalists. For the full anti-treaty argument, written by Belmont, see Congress, House, *Participation of the United States in the Congo Conference,* 48th Cong., 2d sess., H.R. Report 2655 (1885). One may suspect that, in addition to the arguments for and against, there was a deep, underlying element of partisanship—President Arthur's administration was Republican; Cleveland and Belmont were Democrats.

Nevertheless, the concern of the United States with what was happening in Africa and the policy of the government to maintain the rights of its citizens in Africa were matters that transcended temporary mutations of party politics; the "outward thrust" from the United States was becoming too powerful to be restrained by a tradition of isolationism that even then was beginning to lose its vitality.

As ancient as the tradition and policy of political isolation was the tradition that the government should aid and foster foreign commerce. American industries were growing with tremendous speed; though numerous merchants and other businessmen undoubtedly regarded the domestic market as capable of indefinite expansion, there were many others who foresaw a time when the United States would no longer be able to absorb all the products of American mills, factories, and farms. In addition, as the railway network approached completion and heavy industry no longer needed capital from London or Amsterdam, American capitalists and entrepreneurs began to think of overseas investment opportunities that promised greater returns than domestic loans.

In spite of political isolation and the concentration of the American people upon domestic affairs, there was considerable latent interest in Africa, and particularly in the possibilities offered by the still-unknown country of the Congo. Even before the flurry occasioned by the Berlin Conference, this interest had manifested itself in the mission assigned to Commodore Robert W. Shufeldt in 1878.

In command of the U.S.S. *Ticonderoga*, he was directed by the Secretary of the Navy to proceed first to Liberia, where he would, if necessary, act as umpire in the boundary dispute between Liberia and Great Britain. He would next "visit both the western and eastern coasts of Africa and hold such intercourse with the natives to whom he could obtain access as would enable them to appreciate the advantages of trade with the United States." He was also instructed to visit Madagascar and other places around the world, all with a view to promoting American foreign commerce.[11]

In the course of her cruise down the west coast of Africa, the *Ticonderoga* touched at the mouth of Gabon, where Shufeldt ob-

---

[11] Department of the Navy, *Annual Report of the Secretary of the Navy for the Fiscal Year Ending June 30, 1880* (1880), p. 27.

served with approval the activities of the American missionaries and spent several days at Fernando Póo. In May, 1879, the ship anchored in the Congo River, "the first American ship of war which can be said to have really entered the Congo—the others having anchored at its mouth off Shark's point." From the anchorage, Lieutenant Francis J. Drake and Paymaster William J. Thomson investigated the commercial possibilities of the region. They found that millions of dollars' worth of such raw materials as ivory, palm oil, rubber, sesamum oil, gum copal, groundnuts, and orcin were being exported annually from the river; at the same time vast amounts of cotton goods, liquors, gunpowder, brass rods and rings, and all sorts of metal utensils were being imported. The only article of American production coming into the Congo was tobacco, and it was being imported by Dutch and British—not American—traders. Drake's brief survey, moreover, led him to believe that the country was well adapted to the cultivation of almost anything that could be raised in southern Europe.

In spite of the generally optimistic tone of the reports submitted by Drake and Thomson, Commodore Shufeldt was skeptical about any commercial possibilities for Americans in the Congo. He reported, in substance, that Dutch traders established at Banana, near the mouth of the river, were so firmly entrenched that any effort to break their monopoly would be virtually hopeless. Those same Dutch traders, scenting a threat to themselves and their trade in the *Ticonderoga's* arrival, had but poorly concealed their animosity toward Shufeldt and his officers and crew.[12]

To the average American, however, the commercial possibilities of tribal Africa were secondary to another interest. The last few decades of the nineteenth century saw a resurrection of the missionary fervor of the earlier years. Africa had been a major focus for American missionary effort, and the publication of Stanley's sensational accounts of cannibalism and even more unspeakable depravities kindled the desire of evangelical Christians in both Europe and America to carry the Gospel to that benighted region.

---

[12] See Shufeldt's reports to the Secretary of the Navy, May 21, June 3, June 19, and June 20, 1879, in the Robert W. Shufeldt Papers, 1864–1884, Naval Historical Foundation Collection, on deposit in the Library of Congress. See also "The Congo Commission," *Bradstreet's*, X (1884), 146.

American missionaries had, of course, been prominent in Africa since the inception of the missionary movement, but no missionary, European or American, had ever penetrated into the wilderness of the Congo basin before the 1870's. Once it became known that the Congo valley could be entered via the river's mouth, evangelical associations quickly responded to the opportunity. The first to make the attempt were missionaries sent out from England in 1878 by a group of dissenter philanthropists. Calling themselves the Livingstone Inland Mission, they pioneered simultaneously with the hard-bitten adventurers who under Stanley's direction were cutting roads and establishing stations for the International Association as it was staking its claims to sovereignty. By 1884 the Livingstone Inland Mission had succeeded in setting up a thin chain of missionary stations along the south bank of the river as far up as Stanley Pool. They suffered heavy casualties from disease and also were handicapped by bitter disagreements with Stanley, who had seized their steamboat for use in his expedition to rescue Emin Pasha.[13]

By 1884 the philanthropic group that sponsored and supported the Livingstone Inland Mission was in financial difficulties, and the missions themselves were not prospering in their work as much as had been hoped. In that year the American Baptist Missionary Union's offer to take over the work was gladly accepted. The American Baptist Missionary Union was an old, well-established organization which had developed a policy very different from that of the Livingstone Inland Mission. The Livingstone missionaries conducted their work in several languages and regions; the Americans preferred to concentrate initially in a central mission using one language and from this base to extend their efforts gradually, one step at a time. From the central mission the Baptists branched out to a circle of satellite stations and eventually advanced to new regions.[14]

For some years the Baptists and the Disciples of Christ, who

---

[13] Ruth M. Slade, *English-speaking Missions in the Congo Independent State (1878–1908)* (Brussels, 1959), pp. 32–77.

[14] Shortly after taking over, the American Baptists closed one remote station and turned another over to a Swedish missionary organization. A few years later still another detached station, at Balenge on the equator, seven hundred miles from the mouth of the Congo, was turned over to a Disciples of Christ mission from the United States.

maintained a single mission, were the sum total of American missionary efforts in the Congo. During the 1880's Bishop William Taylor and, later, Bishop Joseph C. Hartzell, of the Methodist Episcopal Church, investigated the Congo with the idea of establishing a chain of Methodist missions, but the plans were not destined to come to fruition during the nineteenth century.

After the Baptists, the next major American missionary effort in the Congo was undertaken by the Southern Presbyterian Church, prodded originally by a young Negro minister, William H. Sheppard. A native of Virginia and a graduate of Hampton Institute and Tuscaloosa Theological Institute, Sheppard had aspired from childhood to be a missionary to Africa. Shortly after his ordination in 1887, he approached the mission office of his church, which was, however, reluctant to send him to Africa alone. In 1890 a second volunteer presented himself—the Reverend Samuel N. Lapsley, of Anniston, Alabama. That same year the two young ministers, one white, the other Negro, set out for the Congo, to explore for a site where they might commence their missionary labors.[15]

Traveling together, the two young men had adventures comparable to any that befell other explorers in a harsh and unknown country. Lapsley died of an African fever, like so many Europeans and Americans before him. Undiscouraged, Sheppard continued alone. On one occasion his life was spared by suspicious tribesmen because, somehow, they believed that he was the reincarnation of a legendary chief (he took care not to disillusion them at that time). Eventually he established himself at Luebo, deep in the interior, in a region never before penetrated by any missionary. Before his final return to America, many years later, he had the satisfaction of seeing the mission he had founded attracting converts by the hundreds and growing and expanding until it was one of the most important centers of Christianity and civilization in Central Africa.[16]

The Baptists and the Presbyterians virtually complete the story of American missionary efforts in the Congo during the nineteenth century. The Disciples of Christ, at the station at Balenge which they

---

[15] William H. Sheppard, *Pioneers in Congo* (Louisville, Ky., n.d.), pp. 11–15.

[16] *Ibid.*, pp. 91–157; Johannes du Plessis, *The Evangelisation of Pagan Africa* (Cape Town, 1930), pp. 216–221.

had taken over from the Baptists, experienced many misfortunes, including the inevitable deaths from fever, and did not become firmly established until the very end of the century; the story of their work in the Congo belongs properly to the twentieth century.

During the 1880's and early 1890's the attitude of the American people was changing, and the traditions of isolation and noninvolvment were gradually ceasing to be regarded as immutable laws. When a second conference to discuss the Congo and African affairs was assembled at Brussels in 1890, the United States took part without arousing the flurry of opposition that had attended participation in the Berlin Conference. The American delegate was Henry S. Sanford, who had left Leopold's service and was selected because of his familiarity with the diplomatic and legal problems of the Congo. The original Berlin Convention was amended slightly so as to enable Leopold's government in Africa to raise needed revenue by charging nondiscriminatory tonnage and duties, and a further agreement was adopted which it was hoped would restrict the traffic in liquor and firearms.

After the Brussels Conference, United States official diplomatic interest in Africa subsided for the rest of the century. But no account of the United States and the Congo is complete without mention of Richard Dorsey Mohun. Ever since the recognition of the Congo Free State, it had been the policy of the United States to maintain a commercial agent there as the American representative, and in 1892 Mohun was appointed to the position. He went to Africa by way of Brussels, where he paid his respects to King Leopold, the sovereign of the Free State, of whose determination to bring peace and civilization to the Congo he became convinced.

Since trade between the United States and the new state was still almost nonexistent, Mohun began to investigate the commercial potentialities of the country, and this entailed exploration. He traveled into areas that no Westerner had previously penetrated, and the dangers involved seem to have been meat and drink to him. Among his earlier reports to the State Department is one that is extraordinary among official dispatches but may be taken as typical of Mohun:

I desired to see the natives making cloth, and asked permission of the chief to visit the town, which was readily granted.

64

I took only six men with me armed with revolvers under their shirts. When I had gotten about ten minutes distance from the town I was most foully attacked from the bush with spears and poisoned arrows. Fortunately none of my men were struck, and before they could throw their arrows again we opened fire. We captured the village and I burned it to the ground to teach them a lesson. This is only one of five or six times I have been compelled to fight during the past six months.

The whole eastern boundary of the State is now shut by the Arabs, and all the white men who were in the different posts have been killed. Their bodies were afterwards eaten by the large number of cannibal slaves attached to the caravans.[17]

The latter part of Mohun's statement refers to the fact that the Congo Free State authorities had suddenly found themselves involved in a savage war with the Arab slave traders from the east coast who were established well within the boundaries of the state and who were bitterly resentful of the efforts that were being made to suppress their lucrative commerce. Such a war was regarded in Europe and America as a struggle between barbarism and civilization—between slavers and the heralds of peace and freedom. The Congo forces were heavily outnumbered by the Arabs and their native allies, and when Mohun was asked to serve in the place of a Belgian officer who was seriously ill, he did not hesitate to join the conflict. In a short time he was acting as chief of artillery for the Free State, and in this capacity he took a leading part in most of the battles.[18]

Before the war was ended, with the complete defeat of the Arabs, the Free State authorities sent a strong exploring party to determine the practicability of a water route from Lake Tanganyika to the Lualaba River (the upper Congo), with Mohun as second in command. When the Belgian commander of the expedition fell ill, Mohun took charge and continued in full command until the expedition completed its task.

The oddest feature of Mohun's career is the fact that the United

---

[17] Mohun to the State Department, December 23, 1892, quoted in Cyrus Townsend Brady, Jr., *Commerce and Conquest in East Africa, with Particular Reference to the Salem Trade with Zanzibar* (Salem, Mass., 1950), pp. 200–201.

[18] The Richard Dorsey Mohun Papers, National Archives, Washington, D.C. See also Mohun, "The Death of Emin Pasha," *Century Magazine*, XLIX (1894–1895), 591–598.

States government, of which he was the accredited official representative, never took the slightest exception to his extraordinary, highly undiplomatic activities. The State Department evidently was satisfied by his explanation that he refused to accept pay from the Congo Free State for his services as an officer. Far from disavowing Mohun and his actions, the government seemed to approve; after his return to the United States upon the completion of his term of office, he was appointed to the still-important post of consul at Zanzibar—a promotion that he would not have received had he been *persona non grata*. He remained at Zanzibar for three years; he then resigned from the service of the United States and devoted the remainer of his life to Africa and the Congo Free State. Mohun led exploring parties into Katanga, verifying rumors of fabulous mineral wealth in that region, and later travelers encountered him busily constructing telegraph lines through the wilderness.[19]

With Mohun the more spectacular part played by Americans in opening the region comes to an end. From that time until the present, Americans have continued to take part in the affairs of the Congo, but their roles have been prosaic in comparison with those of Stanley, Mohun, and the Negro missionary, Sheppard. Few Americans today are aware of the prominence of their compatriots in bringing knowledge of the hidden recesses of Central Africa to the rest of the world. Before Stanley's incredible voyage down the vast river, inner Africa was the land of Rider Haggard's romances—a lost world where any day the impossible might become reality. After Stanley and his helpers and successors, inner Africa became almost as familiar as the prairies of Kansas. The Americans who assisted in opening the Congo were filling roles in the tradition of Daniel Boone, John C. Frémont, and the many other pioneers who subdued the wilds of North America.

---

[19] Mohun Papers, *passim;* Brady, *Commerce and Conquest in East Africa,* pp. 113, 209–210; Isaac F. Marcosson, *An African Adventure* (New York and London, 1921), pp. 245–246; Demetrius C. de K. Boulger, *The Congo State; or The Growth of Civilization in Central Africa* (London, 1898), pp. 316–317. Leopold made Mohun a Chevalier of the "Royal Order of the Lion of the Congo" for his services in the Arab war—an honor which he accepted subject to the approval of his own government.

CHAPTER 5

Traders and Soldiers of Misfortune

Throughout the nineteenth century, American interest in eastern Africa centered on Zanzibar, the commercial focal point for the entire region. Americans were the first to seize the opportunities then offered by the potentialities and changing conditions on the eastern coast. In the years just preceding the Civil War, the commerce of Zanzibar was largely dominated by American merchants and traders, whose goods filled the shops and bazaars. The Africans of adjacent continental areas dressed themselves in *merikani,* refusing to accept substitutes from Manchester or Madras. Ivory hunters preferred American hatchets. Ships flying the Stars and Stripes crowded the ports and anchorages.[1] The commercially minded ruler, Sultan Seyyid Said, finding that trade within his dominions was handicapped by the lack of small coins, ordered a supply from the United States. When he decided to engage in a trading venture of his own, his ship was dispatched to the United States.[2]

The Civil War, as discussed earlier, struck this commerce and influence a body blow. The American merchants at Zanzibar, struggling hard, managed to survive commercially. To retain their customers they had to substitute goods of British or German manufacture for the usual American goods, and their cargoes were transported to Africa under the British, French, or Hanseatic flags. They maintained their credit, but their businesses inevitably declined before the end of the war, while competitors took full advantage of the opportunity

---

[1] F. B. Pearce, *Zanzibar, the Island Metropolis of Eastern Africa* (London, 1920), pp. 133–134.

[2] Letter, from the Reverend R. O. Hume to the American Board, July 3, 1839, *Missionary Herald,* XXXVI (1840), 60; Hermann Frederick Eilts, "Ahmad Bin Na'aman's Mission to the United States in 1840: The Voyage of *Al-Sultanah* to New York City," *Essex Institute Historical Collections,* XCVIII (1962), 218–277.

that was thus offered to them of promoting their own interests.[3]

For several years after the war the Americans seemed to be recovering their position, against the fierce competition of British, Indian, German, and French traders who had profited from American inability to satisfy African wants during the war. In 1869 Robert S. Rantoul, the collector of customs at Salem (the port most deeply concerned with African trade), said, somewhat oratorically, that "a large fraction of the dates, gums, spices, ivory, ebony, sheep skins and goat skins brought into this country" and "the delicious Arabian coffee, the aromatic berry of Mocha," were again passing through Salem.[4]

In spite of the revival, conditions were taking an unfavorable turn for American merchants in East Africa. The opening of the Suez Canal in 1869 and the replacement of sail by steam-power craft reduced shipping costs and time so that European goods could be sold more cheaply than American. The typical American sailing vessel could not compete with the larger, faster ships from England and Germany. One by one, most of the merchants and merchant firms that had supplied East Africa with American cotton cloth, tools, and trinkets closed their Zanzibar offices and went out of business.

The American commercial interest did not, however, entirely lapse. The Africans still preferred American cotton goods to all others; the bulk of the gum copal gathered annually found its way to the factories of New England; and until well into the twentieth century the greater part of the ivory of East Africa was carried to the United States. The fact that commerce is a two-edged weapon is illustrated by the ivory trade. In 1882, when the supply of ivory was cut off by tribal warfare in Tanganyika, many persons in Connecticut suffered severely as factories closed down and employees were thrown out of work, much as had happened in England when the Civil War cut off the supply of cotton.[5]

---

[3] The decline is evident in the shipping statistics. In 1859 American shipping entering Zanzibar amounted to 10,890 tons—more than the combined tonnage of all other countries—and in 1866, before the postwar recovery began, it was only 2,515 tons. See Reginald Coupland, *The Exploitation of East Africa, 1856–1890* (London, 1939), pp. 78–79.

[4] Robert S. Rantoul, "The Port of Salem," *Essex Institute Historical Collections*, X (1869), 72; see also Norman Robert Bennett, "Americans in Zanzibar, 1865–1915," *Essex Institute Historical Collections*, XCVIII (1962), 36.

[5] Ernest D. Moore, *Ivory, Scourge of Africa* (New York and London, 1931), pp. 116–117.

Even though American commerce with Zanzibar and its dominions declined to a fraction of the volume before the Civil War, there was still enough to justify maintaining a consul at Zanzibar. In the days before the consular service was a career branch of the government service, a consular office cost the government very little. The salary was extremely small; a consul was expected to support himself from the fees and other perquisites that went with the office. At Zanzibar the United States consul was almost invariably one of the merchants residing and doing business there. Moreover, the consulate at Zanzibar came to be regarded as the just prerogative of certain Salem traders and merchant families, and there was considerable resentment when an outsider was appointed. Three successive holders of the office will serve to illustrate. In 1865, Edward D. Ropes, of Salem, was appointed; he was succeeded in 1869 by Francis Ropes Webb, of Salem, who in turn was succeeded in 1872 by John F. Webb, also of Salem.[6]

Since the consul at Zanzibar was the only official American representative in the Sultan's dominions, his duties were diplomatic as well as commercial, but in actual fact his diplomatic duties were negligible. On only one occasion in the period after the Civil War did the consulate attain, for a brief time, some political importance. As a result of British determination to suppress the slave trade on the East African coast, Great Britain had in 1845 obtained a treaty from the Sultan under which the export of slaves from his African territories was banned but the shipment of slaves from the mainland to Zanzibar and Pemba, and between the islands, was authorized. Since it was almost impossible to prove that a dhow loaded with slaves was really going to Muscat or Persia if the master asserted that his destination was Zanzibar or Pemba, the enforcement of the treaty was extremely difficult. Beginning about 1868, the Royal Navy intensified its campaign against the illegal slave trade, at times in a manner unquestionably highhanded and arbitrary. Francis R. Webb, who had been in business in Zanzibar for years and who was later appointed American consul, estimated that the British sank or burned at least seventy Arab craft, many of which, he believed, were innocent of any

---

[6] Brady, *Commerce and Conquest in East Africa,* p. 113; letter, January 31, 1964, from the National Archives to the authors.

part in the slave trade. It was Webb's fear that the British meant eventually to abolish slavery itself—not merely the overseas trade in slaves—and that this outcome would injure business.[7] In 1868 he went so far as to urge the State Department to send an American warship to Zanzibar as a preventive measure. Washington, however, took a broader view, and the reply to Webb's request was actually a sharp reprimand for even suggesting opposition to the British policy: "So far from protesting against it, the influence of this government would be exerted in its favor."[8]

The abuses in British anti-slave-trade activities were corrected shortly by the establishment of a vice-admiralty court at Zanzibar, with John Kirk as both British consul and justice of the court. Kirk was a noted African explorer in his own right. He had been in Africa since the 1850's, when he was a member of Dr. Livingstone's expedition to explore the Zambesi River. He was grimly determined to put a stop to the traffic in human beings. But Kirk entertained something of the contempt for traders and merchants that has been characteristic of numerous British colonial officials; he had also an innate dislike and suspicion of Americans. There was a clash of personalities between Kirk and some of the Americans in Zanzibar, including Consul Francis R. Webb. Kirk, moreover, was deeply imbued with the idea of promoting and advancing the British Empire and with enhancing British prestige. This was an attitude that could not make for smooth personal relations in the tiny foreign community in Zanzibar, where most of the Europeans and Americans were traders or merchants and were at all times deeply suspicious of British motives.

In 1872 Her Majesty's Government decided to clarify the situation at Zanzibar by dispatching Sir Bartle Frere to persuade the Sultan to modify the treaty of 1845 and stop the intradominion shipment of slaves—the subterfuge under which thousands of slaves were illegally transported out of Africa every year. On March 6, 1872, Sir Edward Thornton, the British Minister at Washington, addressed a lengthy note to Secretary of State Hamilton Fish, calling attention to the horrors and ravages of the slave trade in the interior of East Africa, as revealed in numerous reports and explorers' accounts, and

[7] Bennett, "Americans in Zanzibar, 1865–1915," p. 37.
[8] *Ibid.*, p. 38.

the need for cooperation of the other great powers to end the slave trade.[9] In addition to abrogating the objectionable provisions of the treaty, Great Britain suggested governmental support of steamship and mail service to East Africa as a means of fostering legitimate trade—and in the intellectual climate of the time, legitimate trade was almost synonymous with civilization.

The Secretary of State cautiously refused to commit the United States to any common or joint action with another power, but, in view of the praiseworthy objective of British policy, the United States consul at Zanzibar would be instructed to "intimate to the sovereign of that country that we would be glad to see that provision of the treaty between him and Great Britain terminated." The commander of the first American warship to visit the East African coast would be ordered to carry the same message.[10]

This exchange of notes and information occurred in March, 1872, but governmental business was then conducted in a leisurely way, and the matter was in abeyance for some time. All summer the U.S.S. *Yantic* lay in the dockyard, undergoing repairs and refitting in preparation for sailing to the Asiatic station via the Suez Canal. Not until several days after she sailed did anyone realize that she would pass not too far from Zanzibar on her voyage. On September 3, five days after the *Yantic* had departed, the Navy Department cabled the necessary instructions to the United States consul at Gibraltar, to be transmitted to Commander Byron Wilson when the ship arrived there. The *Yantic* was not a fast vessel, and it was the end of October before Secretary Fish was able to inform Sir Edward Thornton that Wilson had received orders to proceed to Zanzibar and cooperate with Frere's mission to the Sultan.[11]

The *Yantic* anchored at Zanzibar in January, 1873, several days ahead of the arrival of Sir Bartle Frere and his staff. Commander Wilson embraced his diplomatic assignment with enthusiasm. Hoping to emulate "Stanley and Livingstone over again," he immediately composed a "long and strong dispatch" for the Sultan. Himself a Union veteran of the American Civil War, Wilson urged the Sultan

---

[9] *Foreign Relations, 1872–1873*, pp. 208–210.
[10] *Ibid.*, pp. 210–211.
[11] *Ibid.*, pp. 214–215.

to follow the lead of "the last among the great civilized nations to abolish slavery as an institution in their midst."[12]

Wilson hoped to be able to present an accomplished fact to the British mission when they arrived, but he did not reckon on the opposition—even active hostility—of his own country's consul. The acting consul, John F. Webb, seems to have believed that Frere's mission was simply a British scheme to drive out business competitors. Whether with Webb's knowledge or not, the consulate's interpreter, in translating Wilson's communication into Arabic, so emasculated it that the commander seemed actually to be urging the Sultan to stand firm in resisting changes.

As for Webb, he would have nothing to do with the matter beyond advising the Sultan to uphold the treaty of 1845. Amazing though it may be, this was the way he interpreted his instructions from Washington. Having given this advice, he considered that he had complied with his orders. He refused to back up Wilson in any way and declined all cooperation with Frere's mission, going even to the rude and inexcusable extreme of refusing to return the courtesy calls of the mission's members.

Fortunately for the reputation of the United States, Acting Consul John F. Webb became ill, and Francis Ropes Webb resumed the consulate. Although he had been lukewarm in his support of previous antislavery measures, his point of view was much more realistic than was his kinsman's, and he recognized that slavery and the slave trade were ultimately doomed. As a result, when Sir Bartle Frere gave the Sultan an ultimatum—either he would consent to the revised treaty, or Zanzibar would be blockaded—the American consul was foremost among those advising the Sultan to comply at once.[13]

Aside from this somewhat disagreeable episode, the United States consulate at Zanzibar during the latter part of the nineteenth century was almost entirely a commercial office. Consul Francis R. Webb assisted Stanley's preparations for his expedition in search of Livingstone. Otherwise he and his successors were called upon to do little beyond furthering their own businesses and signing consular papers.

American merchants continued their struggles to win the com-

---

[12] Quoted in Coupland, *The Exploitation of East Africa,* p. 193.
[13] Bennett, "Americans in Zanzibar, 1865–1915," pp. 41–44.

merce of Zanzibar and East Africa through the 1870's and managed to secure most of the gum copal and ivory. The Africans continued to prefer American cotton cloth to all others. But there were difficulties. In 1872 a disastrous storm—the worst in local recorded history—caused such damage that the economy of Zanzibar and of all of East Africa was disrupted. Many African middlemen were unable to meet their obligations, and as a result one American firm was forced out of business, unable either to pay its creditors or to collect from its debtors. Other American firms, somewhat more resilient because of working arrangements with the leading Indian merchants, managed to survive but were badly hurt. American business at Zanzibar was aided, however, by the introduction of kerosene for lighting. Kerosene was cheaper for this purpose than the locally produced animal and vegetable oils and was made especially attractive when the promoters of the new industry in America furnished a serviceable lamp at a price even the poorest could afford.[14]

Nevertheless, American predominance in the commerce of Zanzibar was being undermined. The Suez Canal, along with the advantages in cost and speed that it gave to European shipping, brought increasing numbers of British and German merchants to the eastern coast of Africa—particularly the Germans. In addition to cutthroat competition, the American merchants had to fight continually against the prejudice and dislike of that master empire builder John Kirk, who had quickly become the power behind the Sultan's throne. Kirk never missed an opportunity to discredit Americans and threw every possible obstacle in their way. Thus, a petition to the Sultan by a group of merchants of several nationalities, urging new regulations to improve the efficiency and operation of caravans, was made by him to seem an underhanded attempt by the Americans to revive the slave trade, and in consequence the American consul received an unwarranted and unjust reprimand from Washington. An illegal search of an American ship by the Royal Navy and the arbitrary removal of two Negro crew members on the grounds that they were slaves, in spite of the captain's firm denial, were strongly supported by Kirk, who took this occasion to make a sweeping charge that "American officials and others in these parts are in the habit of buy-

14 *Ibid.*, pp. 45–47.

ing slaves." In other ways, too, he went out of his way to be disagreeable to the Americans and to exhibit his contempt for such miserable creatures, while Kirk's successor, Euan-Smith, referred to the American consul as a "vulgar pushing fellow anxious to make his position felt in Zanzibar politics."[15]

It would be incorrect to speak of the end of American trade with Zanzibar and East Africa, for it has never ended; but one by one the old American firms found it expedient to close their Zanzibar offices and discontinue their efforts to survive in the African trade. As Great Britain and Germany absorbed the dominions of the Sultan of Zanzibar into their colonial empires, merchants and traders of other nations were quietly, but decisively, pushed aside. Yet the period of American dominance in commerce and shipping at Zanzibar and other East African ports had results that cannot be measured, or even estimated, by commercial statistics. Concentrated as it was—in a few New England ports which otherwise would have been of minor importance—the East African trade created capital that contributed directly to the development of other areas and resources within the United States. A large part of the financing of railroad construction in the Far West was furnished by New England capital that sought opportunities for investment after the African trade declined. Moreover, it is not unreasonable to ascribe to the African trade, along with such ventures as whaling expeditions into the unknown and dangerous Arctic and Antarctic seas, one of the sources of the tradition that made the New England merchant and entrepreneur willing to take long—though carefully considered—chances. Many of the men who changed American business into "big business" in the last decades of the nineteenth century were Yankees—and the shipmasters who trafficked on remote African shores where few others would venture had come from the same part of the United States.

Although the Civil War marked the beginning of the decline of American commercial supremacy in East Africa, it led indirectly to a period of activity by Americans in the upper valley of the Nile and in the Sudan. The end of the war left a large number of Americans with their taste for adventure and a military life still unsated and with little opportunity to gratify it in the minuscule United States

[15] Quoted, *ibid.*, p. 59.

Army of the time. The defeat of the Confederacy, too, left many experienced professional soldiers of the South without means of livelihood in the military profession at home. For several years after the war the United States was a reservoir of highly trained, seasoned staff officers and combat commanders.

The availability of such men coincided neatly with a demand for them in Egypt, where the Khedive Ismail aspired to transform the ancient land of the Pharaohs into a great modern empire. To do this, he inaugurated railway projects, built roads, schools, and hospitals, and laid plans to extend the borders of his country into the region of the Central African lakes and the still-unexplored reaches of the Sudan. Further, Ismail wished to be free from interference on the part of his nominal overlord at Constantinople and thus needed to strengthen and modernize his fighting forces. He brought in foreign experts and in the early 1870's took more than thirty Americans into his employment. Not only were the Americans possessed of good professional military qualifications, but also they had the advantage, in the Khedive's eyes, of being untainted by any connection with ambitions or interests in Egypt likely to clash with his own—they could give him their unqualified allegiance and loyalty. And they were more than specialists in combat, for their experience included mapping, surveying, and exploring. In numbers the Americans were about equally divided between former Confederates and former Union soldiers, and about half were graduates of West Point or Annapolis. Five were second lieutenants of the United States Army, permitted by William T. Sherman, the Commanding General of the United States Army, to take indefinite leave of absence for the sake of the practical experience they would gain in Egypt.[16]

---

[16] William B. Hesseltine and Hazel C. Wolf, *The Blue and the Gray on the Nile* (Chicago, 1961), p. 2. Although the United States government officially had nothing to do with the presence of the Americans in Egypt, General Sherman was deeply interested and gave his personal recommendation to many of them, Confederate as well as Union.

The Americans in Ismail's service were not the first of their nationality to wear the uniform of an Egyptian ruler's army. In 1820 and 1821 George Bethune English, native of Massachusetts, graduate of Harvard, former officer of the United States Marine Corps, was chief of artillery in an Egyptian expedition dispatched by Mohammed Ali to destroy the remnants of the Mamelukes and bring the upper valley of the Nile into subjection. English held the rank of general

The head of the American group was Brigadier General Charles P. Stone, a capable, energetic engineer officer to whom the Civil War had brought nothing but professional misfortune. Although a staunch and loyal Unionist, he had the bad luck of losing a minor battle early in the war and, without coming to trial, was practically convicted of treason by the press and the Secretary of War. His consuming ambition was to vindicate his honor, and it may be said that in the judgment of history he achieved this abundantly by his service with the Khedive. Next to General Stone was Brigadier General William W. Loring, a battle-scarred veteran of the Mexican War and numerous Indian campaigns and also a noted explorer of the American Far West. When the Civil War broke out, he resigned from the United States Army and cast his lot with his native South. Early in the conflict, however, he disagreed on a matter of professional judgment with General Thomas Jonathan Jackson—the redoubtable Stonewall Jackson—and this error blocked his advancement in the Confederate Army. Loring was far from being an embittered man, but he also was anxious to rehabilitate his reputation.[17]

Little need be said about the purely Egyptian phases of the work and adventures of the Americans in the Khedive's army. Their intended duties were primarily organization and training; nevertheless, several found themselves in the thick of fighting. In 1875, at Gondet, according to the English general and hero "Chinese" Gordon, an unidentified American commanding a detachment of black troops

officer in the Egyptian forces and had among his soldiers two Americans who had apostatized and become Moslems—as, indeed, English himself had done, at least outwardly. (See George Bethune English, *A Narrative of the Expedition to Dongola and Sennar under the Command of His Excellence Ismael Pasha, Undertaken by Order of His Highness Mehemmed Ali Pasha, Viceroy of Egypt* [Boston, 1823], pp. 15–16, 158, and the article "George Bethune English," by Walter L. Wright, Jr., in the *Dictionary of American Biography.*) English did not consider himself an explorer, yet his description of much of the country through which the army moved is the first modern eyewitness account by an American or European. One of the American soldiers, identified only by his assumed name of Khalil Aga, was reported by English to be the first person to travel the entire length of the Nile from Rosetta to Sennar.

[17] Edward Dicey, in *The Story of the Khedivate* (New York, 1902), p. 257, erroneously credits Stone with having been "an officer of distinction in the Confederate army." Other writers have supposed that several of these Americans were Englishmen.

"made a gallant fight" against an overwhelming body of Abyssinian invaders, until he and his whole force perished under the Abyssinian spears.[18] Loring, probably to his disgust, found himself chief of staff and adviser to an Egyptian prince who commanded a field force sent against the Abyssinians—a prince who was ignorant of the very elements of war, felt no martial enthusiasm, and ignored all advice. When the demoralized prince led in leaving the battlefield, it was Loring who saved the remnants of the command and prevented what was admittedly a defeat from becoming a disaster.

In the same battle, Surgeon Major Thomas D. Johnson, of Tennessee, also a Confederate veteran, was wounded and captured. He was rescued by an Abyssinian *ras* (prince) when at the point of being murdered along with other prisoners. During the forty-odd days of his captivity Johnson was treated as a guest and was finally released, after a long interrogation by King John of Abyssinia and upon his solemn promise to endeavor to deliver a letter which the King wished to send to Queen Victoria without the knowledge of the "Turks" (i.e., the Egyptians).[19] Although many Europeans earlier had close contact with the Abyssinians, Johnson was beyond doubt the first American to observe them intimately and to have a long audience with their ruler. His account of his experiences as a prisoner gives a remarkably balanced and objective view of his captors.

In their efforts to modernize and discipline the Egyptian army, the Americans faced odds too heavy to be overcome. Nevertheless, they accomplished much that was positive in value and has since been largely forgotten:

> When the American officers accepted the invitation of Ismail Pasha the writ of the Khedive did not run throughout the Sudan. The Equatorial Provinces were closed to civilization. Under American leadership the Sudan was won back to Egypt, and during the period of their primacy the Egyptian flag was respected as far south as the Equator.[20]

The significance of these American "soldiers of misfortune" lies

---

[18] George Birkbeck Hill (ed.), *Colonel Gordon in Central Africa, 1874–1879* (2d ed.; London, 1884), p. 205.

[19] "The Egyptian Campaign in Abyssinia, from the Notes of a Staff Officer," *Blackwood's Edinburgh Magazine,* CXXII (1877), 26–39.

[20] Pierre Crabitès, *Americans in the Egyptian Army* (London, 1938), p. 20.

not in their ultimate failure to transform the Egyptian army into a first-class combat force but rather in their blazing of trails into Central Africa that others followed a few years later. Incidental to their military duties, they reconnoitered and mapped thousands of miles of territory that no Western men had ever seen before. Even though their names are little known, or forgotten, and others have received credit for discoveries and explorations actually made by them, these Americans put their stamp upon the Sudan and vast regions to the south of the Sahara. General Loring, in his reminiscences, has recorded some instances:

> Lieutenant Colonel Mason and Colonel Prout navigated and surveyed Lake Albert Nyanza, discovered by Baker in 1864. General Raleigh Colston, formerly an officer of the Southern Confederacy, was more recently one of our American explorers in the interior of Africa. His geological and botanical collections, maps, and reconnaissance add much to the interest of a visit to the Citadel at Cairo. Devoted to duty, he penetrated into the comparatively unknown region between the Debbé, Mantoul, and Obeyail, and far into the provinces of Kordofan and Darfour in Central Africa.[21]

Colston's exploration of Kordofan took place in 1873 and 1874, under orders from the Khedive. It was Colston's second exploration, and came perilously close to being his last. In the heart of Africa he became dangerously ill, so weak as to require assistance to mount his horse, or even to walk, but he stubbornly refused to turn back and struggled on until he reached El Obeid. Too ill to continue, he turned the expedition over to his second in command, Colonel Henry G. Prout, an engineer from the University of Michigan who had had experience in mapping the American West. Prout continued on into Darfur, where he joined up with an expedition under Major Erastus Purdy which had penetrated the region from another direction. Meanwhile, contrary to all expectations, including his own, Colston was recovering. His labors resulted in a substantial volume which provided the world with accurate and scientific knowledge concerning a part of Africa previously known only to legend.[22]

---

[21] William Wing Loring, *A Confederate Soldier in Egypt* (New York, 1884), p. 298.

[22] See Crabitès, *Americans in the Egyptian Army,* pp. 64–90, and Hesseltine

Americans were responsible for other explorations and surveys worthy of note. Major Oscar Eugene Fechet, of Michigan, who was one of the lieutenants granted indefinite leave of absence by General Sherman, conducted surveys in Nubia and the Sudan and designated Aswan as the most suitable site for a great dam to control the waters of the Nile. Major William P. A. Campbell, a former Confederate naval officer, took part in the exploration of the desert between Berenice, on the Red Sea, and Berber, on the Nile. He became fluent in Arabic and in 1874 accompanied General Gordon to Khartoum, where he died of cholera. Lieutenant Colonel Alexander McComb Mason, a graduate of Annapolis who had served in the Confederate Navy, was initially placed in charge of the Khedive's steamers on the Nile, since there was no Egyptian navy. Such an assignment was too restrictive for his boundless energy, and he soon joined the ranks of the explorers. Mason discovered the Semliki River flowing into Lake Albert and proved that the waters that fed the Albert Nile came from the deep heartland of Africa. He also established and mapped the exact configuration of Lake Albert and determined its true extent— geographical details of considerable importance.[23]

Other spectacular and important contributions to geographical knowledge came from the activities of Colonel Charles Chaillé-Long.[24] The hyphen which he habitually inserted in his name has led

---

and Wolf, *The Blue and the Gray on the Nile*, pp. 120–148.

Colston's *Rapport sur les régions centrales et nordiques du Kordofán* was published in 1875 and Prout's *General Report on the Province of Kordofan* in 1877, both at Cairo. Colston, a brigadier general in the Confederate Army during the war, was primarily an educator, having been a professor at the Virginia Military Institute. He had come to Egypt for the purpose of organizing an Egyptian military academy along lines similar to those of West Point and V.M.I., but he was instead given the role of field geologist, botanist, and explorer. The Colston Papers are at the University of North Carolina Library, which also has the papers of other Americans who served in Egypt.

[23] Crabitès, *Americans in the Egyptian Army*, pp. 214–227. Fechet's *Journal of the March of an Expedition in Nubia between Assouan and Abouhamed . . . 1873* was published in Cairo in 1878. Mason's *Report on a Reconnaissance of Lake Albert* was published in 1878 as Vol. XXII of the *Proceedings* of the Royal Geographical Society, London. Mason was a descendant of a signer of the Declaration of Independence and was closely related to several men who have been distinguished in the affairs of the United States, particularly in the armed forces.

[24] The Chaillé-Long Papers are held by the Library of Congress.

some writers to assume that he was an Englishman, but Chaillé-Long was a native of the Eastern Shore of Maryland. He was a college student when the Civil War broke out; most of his relatives and friends "went south," but Chaillé-Long entered the Union Army and finished the war as a captain. The end of hostilities found him enthusiastically looking for further adventure and military life. Consequently, when he was offered the chance for a commission in the Khedive's army, he jumped at it. In 1870 he was commissioned a colonel, and when the famous General Gordon arrived in Egypt in 1874, Chaillé-Long was designated his chief of staff by the Egyptian War Ministry.[25]

Shortly after arriving in Equatoria with Gordon, Chaillé-Long was dispatched upon a mission to the King of Uganda. After innumerable adventures and a great deal of hardship, he finally reached Uganda and, according to his own account, concluded a treaty with M'Tesa by which the King acknowledged Egyptian overlordship. The political mission, however, was probably the least significant part of Chaillé-Long's journey. On his return, fighting his way through attacking tribesmen on several occasions, he traversed a portion of the Nile never before explored by a white man and discovered Lake Kioga, which was previously unknown. Gordon, writing to his sister from Gondokoro on September 11, 1874, remarked that for more than six months he had not heard from Long, who had gone to Uganda. Six weeks later, Gordon wrote:

> Long came in the day before yesterday. He has had a hard time of it. He left this place for Fatiko on April 24; got there in ten days, and from thence went on to Karuma Falls. . . . He went to Mtesa and got a very good reception. He went down to Urundongani, and thence, with two canoes, descended the Nile to Foweira. He found no cataracts at all on the route. . . . Long says he passed through a large lake between Urundongani and Foweira. He was attacked by Kaba Rega's men and had to fight his way through near Mrooli.[26]

In 1875, after other adventures in the meantime, Chaillé-Long

---

[25] Charles Chaillé-Long, *My Life in Four Continents* (London, 1912), I, 65–67. There was some opposition by British officials in Egypt to Chaillé-Long's initial appointment, on the grounds that such a position should be held by an Englishman, but Gordon himself insisted upon an American.

[26] Quoted in Hill (ed.), *Colonel Gordon in Central Africa*, pp. 54–55; see also Chaillé-Long, *My Life in Four Continents*, pp. 90–111.

was assigned to command the Egyptian land forces in an amphibious operation in the Indian Ocean. To obviate some of the difficulties of communication between Cairo and Equatoria via the Nile, and probably encouraged by Gordon's advice, the Khedive decided to establish an Egyptian base in what is now southern Somalia.[27] The expedition sailed from Suez on September 18, 1875, and on October 16 and 17 landed at the mouth of the Juba River without any opposition. As a precaution, Chaillé-Long seized the antiquated Portuguese fort, held by a nominal Zanzibari garrison, and occupied the slave-trading port of Kismayu (Chisimaio), liberating more than five hundred slaves.

The port and the territory occupied were within the domains claimed by the Sultan of Zanzibar, and it was only a matter of time before that potentate took action. Even though he graciously provided one of the expedition's ships with coal and sent a present of fresh fruits and other supplies to Chaillé-Long, he also promptly sent a cablegram to Great Britain: "Egyptian pirates have seized my army and country and massacred my people. Come to my aid." Since it was no part of Great Britain's policy to permit Egyptian expansion into areas in which British commercial interests were expanding (or hopeful of expanding), immediate pressure was applied upon the Khedive, and the Juba River expedition was withdrawn.[28]

Chaillé-Long resigned his Egyptian commission in 1877. Except for a brief period of conspicuous and distinguished service as American consular agent at Alexandria at the time of the British bombardment in 1882, he had no further concern with Africa, although he lived a long and adventurous life.[29]

After the British occupation of Egypt in 1882, the Americans gradually departed from the Nile and vanished from Egyptian affairs. During the last quarter of the nineteenth century, the great colonial powers of Europe carved up most of Africa among themselves. The United States, except for participating in the Berlin Conference of 1884–1885 and the Brussels Conference of 1890, remained aloof from

---

[27] *My Life in Four Continents*, pp. 146–147.

[28] *Ibid.*, pp. 173–195.

[29] Chaillé-Long's achievements in Africa remained unrecognized by geographers and historians until recent years. This may have been due largely to his unfortunate egoism, arrogance, and habit of "carrying a chip on his shoulder."

African affairs. The few Americans who went to Africa were there quite unofficially and on their own. There were no massive subscription drives to outfit exploring expeditions, nor was there any official organization to represent the government's interest or to advance money and add prestige.

Nevertheless, popular interest in African affairs produced the journalist-explorer, a characteristically American phenomenon. The greatest was Stanley, but in 1887 Stanley disappeared into the African interior to rescue Emin Pasha, the Governor of Egyptian Equatoria. At this juncture, the New York *World*, a bitter rival of Bennett's *Herald*, decided to emulate its enemy by sending an expedition to find Stanley. The *World* dispatched a reporter-adventurer named Thomas Stevens, who had achieved a degree of fame by riding a bicycle around the world and by riding a mustang across the Russian Empire. He was directed to investigate the troubles between the Germans and Arabs in East Africa, look into the slave trade, and find out everything possible regarding the fate of Stanley and Emin. The newspaper authorized Stevens to organize a relief expedition at Zanzibar, as Stanley had done in his search for Livingstone. Stevens led his expedition to the borders of the Masai country (hundreds of miles from where Stanley actually was), but when word reached him that Stanley had reappeared and was en route to Bagamoyo, through territory that had been acquired by Germany, Stevens resolved to be the first person from the outside world to greet him. Outwitting German authorities who forbade him to cross the territory and by a combination of courage, brazen audacity, and pure luck, Stevens finally caught up with and greeted the great explorer. He did not quite achieve his goal of being the first to meet Stanley, for Baron von Gravenreuth, of the German Army, arrived at Stanley's camp ahead of him, but he got there in advance of Frank Vizetelly, correspondent for the New York *Herald*. Stanley was unfeignedly glad to see the two Americans, as well as the German officer, and broke out a bottle of champagne which he had been carefully saving for just such an occasion. Stevens, in his determination to meet Stanley, overcame obstacles and difficulties in a way that Stanley himself could not have improved upon.[30]

---

[30] See Thomas Stevens, *Scouting for Stanley in East Africa* (New York,

An explorer of a different sort was A. Donaldson Smith, of Philadelphia, who led his own expedition from Somaliland into Central Africa in 1894 and 1895. Smith was a wealthy man who was a physician by education and training (he studied medicine at Harvard, Johns Hopkins, and Heidelberg) but a sportsman and a biologist by choice. He wrote:

> The keen love of sport and adventure that is innate in most of the Anglo-Saxon race had always prompted me to go into the remotest corners of the earth, and I suppose it was my seven years medical training in America and Europe which taught me never to lose a chance of doing scientific work when it presented itself.[31]

A hunting trip to Somaliland with a friend inspired Smith to attempt a more extensive expedition, on which he would combine exploration of unknown country with the collection of zoological, botanical, and geological specimens for scientific study. He was wealthy enough to be able to gratify his desires, and in 1894, when he was thirty years of age, he set out from Berbera with a single American companion and a large and carefully equipped expedition. For several months they hunted, botanized, and occasionally fought across Somaliland and southern Abyssinia. Smith made a detailed examination of Lake Stefanie, discovering an unknown smaller lake nearby (which he named Lake Donaldson), and continued westward to Lake Rudolf—a feat that had been considered impossible. Smith and his party returned to the coast along the Tana River, traversing parts of Africa until then unexplored.

Smith's journey through East Africa, while not as epoch making as Stanley's earlier voyage down the Congo, was important scientifically and geographically. His zoological collection included twenty-four previously unknown species of birds, eleven new reptiles, and scores of insects which naturalists had not seen before. He reported

1890), pp. 210–271, and *Africa as Seen by Thomas Stevens and the Hawk-Eye* (Boston, 1890), *passim*. (The "Hawk-Eye" was a camera.) See also H. M. Stanley, *In Darkest Africa; or, The Quest, Rescue, and Retreat of Emin, Governor of Equatoria* (New York, 1890), II, 410.

[31] Arthur Donaldson Smith, *Through Unknown African Countries: The First Expedition from Somaliland to Lake Lamu* (London and New York, 1897), p. 1.

vast reaches of East Africa to be suitable for white colonization and capable of cultivation.[32]

The African mainland was not the only region that attracted the attention of Americans. In 1884 an American naval officer, Lieutenant Mason A. Shufeldt, explored the interior of Madagascar and made what may possibly have been the first crossing of the entire breadth of the island for purely exploratory purposes.

Shufeldt (a son of Commodore Robert W. Shufeldt, who commanded the *Ticonderoga* on her round-the-world voyage of commercial investigation), graduated from the United States Naval Academy in 1873 and had spent most of his sea service in the Far East. He was an officer of the *Ticonderoga* on her voyage, serving under his father's command, and when the ship stopped for some time at Madagascar, he became interested in the island and its problems. He conceived the idea of exploring the unknown interior and wrote to Washington requesting permission to do so. Months later, when he had all but forgotten his request, authorization from the Secretary of the Navy reached him. At that time, in November of 1883, he was on board the U.S.S. *Enterprise*, in Korean waters, and it was not until late in May, 1884, that he was able to reach Tananarive (then known as Antananarivo), the inland capital of the huge island. The Queen's government had received advance notice of his coming, and upon his arrival at the east coast Shufeldt was received by a high official with a letter of welcome.

The eastern part of Madagascar was fairly well known to the world; the western part was little known to Europeans. The tribes of the west were in revolt against the somewhat fumbling efforts of the Queen and her ministers (who were also resisting French aggression at the same time) to extend their authority into that region.[33] The country was disease-ridden, and a powerful slave-trader named Rakatava was bitterly opposed to anything that might interfere with his brutal business there. The few European inhabitants of the capital assured Shufeldt that any attempt to cross to the west coast would be suicidal. Nevertheless, he refused to be deterred, and on May 28,

---

[32] *Ibid.*, pp. 368–374.

[33] Shufeldt, in his account, refers to the Queen and her government as *Hovas*, a term which is now taken to mean the middle class rather than a tribal designation.

1884, with one European companion but at the head of a considerable army of local people, he started. His "army," in addition to 180
bearers whom he hired himself, was increased by some 350 soldiers,
with their families, who were to escort him to the west coast and
remain there as settlers and as a garrison. These people he consented
to command during the march.

The march across the island took almost a full month and involved
the difficulties and hardships that were then an inevitable part of
exploration. Both Shufeldt and his lone white companion nearly succumbed to fever. On at least one occasion Shufeldt, with his revolver,
suppressed a mutiny among his followers. There were several fights
with hostile tribes—presumably Rakatava's followers. The expedition suffered from hunger and found the country destitute of anything
edible. Nevertheless, on June 24, 1884, Shufeldt reached the Mozambique Channel, having traversed regions not described previously by
any European. Dismissing the army, he and his companion hired a
native canoe and two weeks later arrived on the mainland in Mozambique. There they were delighted to see the American flag floating
over the *Sarah Hobart*, of Boston, on which they could return home.

Scientifically, Shufeldt's expedition accomplished little. He formed
the conclusion that the "Zizibongy" (Mania) River could be a commercial channel into the heart of the island and that Madagascar's
potential as a producer of agricultural and mineral products was
enormous.

One or two other features of this nearly forgotten expedition
should be noted. It occurred during a period when the United States
was committed to "isolation" and when foreign commerce was receiving relatively little attention from American businessmen. But the
fact that a naval officer was detached for months from his normal
duties argues that some persons in the United States government
were interested in future possibilities. If not, where did a navy lieutenant get the money to pay his passage from Korea to Madagascar
and hire 180 bearers, buying food for them to consume over a period
of weeks?[34]

---

[34] See Mason A. Shufeldt, "To, about, and across Madagascar," *The United
Service*, XII (January–June, 1885), 1, 506, 691, and XIII (July–December,
1885), 79, 203; in five installments.

It is not certain whether Shufeldt's expedition was the first crossing of

Dr. A. Donaldson Smith and Lieutenant Mason A. Shufeldt by no means complete the roster of Americans who took part in the exploration and opening of East Africa in the latter part of the nineteenth century. They were, however, typical in many respects of the Americans who went to Africa. These men who braved the very real dangers of disease, martial tribes, and wild beasts did not do so because of a duty imposed by their own government and people. They were not building an American empire. The only empire builders among them were such in a limited sense—the Americans who, owing temporary allegiance to the Khedive of Egypt, conscientiously furthered his expansionist policies during their brief years in his service. By far the greater number of the Americans who took part in African affairs were motivated by altruism (as were the missionaries, for example), by the traditional ambition of Americans to better themselves by pioneering, or by the motives which prompted Smith and Shufeldt to leave civilization and venture into the wilds—love of adventure, science, and sport.

Madagascar by a white man. References to the area are difficult to find. The Reverend James Sibree, who was a missionary there for more than half a century, says in his autobiography that in the early times of his missionary work, in the 1860's, the interior was "unexplored and unknown." *Fifty Years in Madagascar: Personal Experience of Mission Life and Work* (London, 1924), p. 64.

Chapter 6

Miners and Adventurers

As the American Far West was reduced to law and order, the farmer replaced the mountain man and trapper, the Indian ceased to be a formidable enemy and became an anachronism secluded in a reservation, and the men who had pushed into the West began to look elsewhere for riches and adventure. To such men, the Dark Continent beckoned alluringly. The gold fields of California were rapidly being worked out, but there were tempting new strikes of gold in Africa, and the hostility of the Matabele warrior or Arab slaver offered an excitement not uninviting to men who had fought Apache or Sioux.

It should not be supposed that high-minded idealists abounded among the Americans who flocked to the southern regions of Africa in the latter part of the nineteenth century. Except for the missionaries, they went there in search of wealth and often were not particular as to the means by which they might achieve success—a characteristic they shared with many men of other nationalities. Their ranks included all sorts. There were educated men and illiterates, devout men and atheists, farmers and sharp city types, bookkeepers and soldiers of fortune.

Whatever their backgrounds, the men who left the United States to search for quick riches in Africa all had this in common: they were tough, mentally and physically. To survive under frontier conditions, to endure hardship and overcome an environment that was often bitterly hostile, required a temperament hard as steel. The idealist had to be as hard as the grossest materialist. The Americans who pioneered in southern Africa, like all other white pioneers on that continent, possessed such hardness in a conspicuous degree.

A gold rush is an international affair. The California gold rush attracted men from every continent. Similarly, the discoveries of gold and diamonds in South Africa drew prospectors from everywhere, including an appreciable number of veteran American prospectors who were still young and vigorous enough to try again. Since the Americans almost alone among the gold seekers had practical experience and know-how, they enjoyed prestige and influence disproportionate to their actual numbers.

During the early 1850's, the white Boer settlers of the newly formed Transvaal Republic, possibly influenced by the discovery of gold in California and in Australia, became mildly interested in the mineral possibilities of their own new country. Consequently, in the autumn of 1853, when Pieter Jacob Marais, who had just returned to Africa from several years' prospecting for gold in California, suggested to the legislative assembly that he be authorized to search for gold mines, his suggestion was eagerly accepted. A contract between the government and Marais was duly signed, and he commenced to prospect. He did not have to look long, since he was in the midst of what would prove to be one of the richest gold fields in the world. On January 7, 1854, Marais exhibited a quantity of gold dust from the Witwatersrand, causing a local sensation. But the discovery was not publicized, and the excitement quickly died down. The Boers, for the most part, wished to live as farmers, and they were not at all anxious to start a movement that would inevitably bring large numbers of Englishmen into their rural Utopia and return them to British rule. The *Graaf Reinet Herald,* on March 4, 1854, commented: "Gold was discovered here a few months ago by Mr. Marais. . . . The Vaal River Government have closed the diggings, until it is decided whether they shall coin their own gold, and whether the Sovereignty will be retained or abandoned by the British Government."[1]

Although gold was discovered in South Africa in 1854, the gold fields did not become important for thirty years. Meanwhile, another mineral began to transform South Africa and drag the subcontinent into the mainstream of world affairs. Before 1867, the major source of the world's supply of diamonds was India, with a few coming occasionally from South America. The accidental discovery in 1867

---

[1] Quoted in James Gray, *Payable Gold: An Intimate Record of the History of the Discovery of the Payable Witwatersrand Goldfields and of Johannesburg in 1886 and 1887* ([Johannesburg], 1937), pp. 17–18.

of a single diamond by a Boer farmer's child was to change the economic destiny of South Africa. The first stone caused no undue excitement. The leading geological and mining savants of Great Britain shook their heads glumly—South Africa was positively not a diamond country. Sir Roderick Murchison, the most eminent geologist of the day, went so far as to say that he would stake his professional reputation on there being no diamond matrix in the country.[2]

The discovery of a second diamond several months later, however, caused an influx of hopeful fortune seekers. As in the California and Australian gold rushes, few actually struck it rich, but some realized their dreams and thereby encouraged others. Among the lucky ones was an Irishman turned American who arrived with the sum of thirty shillings in small coins as his total assets. This amount was speedily exhausted, and he joined the horde of vagrants who drifted from claim to claim, living by their wits. Finally staking a claim at Bulfontein, he formed a partnership with two brothers who had staked a nearby claim—and a few years later the three sold their rights to the newly formed De Beers corporation for a sum in excess of five million pounds.[3] Among the earliest arrivals in 1870 was an American, Jerome L. Babe, whose name still survives in the diamond fields. Babe was in South Africa as a salesman for the Winchester Repeating Arms Company and as a part-time correspondent for the New York *World*. After completing his business at the frontier settlement of Colesberg, he found that he had a few months to spare and decided to try his luck in the diamond fields, which were only some forty miles distant. Babe had had experience as a prospector in California and was unpleasantly impressed with the amount of sheer physical labor in "dry" digging—a process which involved carrying huge amounts of excavated material to the nearest water, or vice versa. To eliminate this, he devised a simple, easily constructed apparatus for the dry screening of the earth and gravel; by the time

---

[2] Alpheus F. Williams, *Some Dreams Come True: Being a Sheaf of Stories Leading up to the Discovery of Copper, Diamonds and Gold in Southern Africa, and of the Pioneers Who Took Part in the Excitement of Those Early Days* (Cape Town, 1948), pp. 57–71.

[3] John Angove, *In the Early Days: The Reminiscences of Pioneer Life on the South African Diamond Fields* (Kimberley and Johannesburg, 1910), pp. 9–10. Angove does not identify this Irishman.

he left the diamond fields a few months later, there were hundreds of the "Yankee Baby"—as it was called—in use, and the "baby" is still used by African prospectors.

Babe was moderately successful in his search for diamonds, but he prospered more by selling diamonds which he bought from miners who needed cash immediately; he also "grubstaked" a number of American and English prospectors and arranged for the purchase of a large tract of land for an American company.[4]

It was in the late 1870's that the presence of gold became widely known, and the gold fields began to attract hordes of prospectors, among them many Americans.[5] In addition, possibly as an accidental by-product of the diamond rush, prospectors in the 1880's began to wash the gravels, looking for gold dust and nuggets when they failed to realize fortunes in gems.

But in due course the surface deposits of South African minerals that attracted independent prospectors were exhausted. To explore, determine, and exploit the deep ore veins and ledges required capital and knowledge far beyond the resources of the "shovel and blanket-roll" prospector. The services of highly trained and experienced geologists, mining engineers, mine managers, and smelter operators were necessary for operations that involved the sinking of shafts hundreds of feet deep, the installation and use of heavy and complex machinery, and the construction of huge industrial plants. In the 1870's and 1880's the United States, the foremost mining country of the world, probably had more expert mining engineers and skilled mine operators than any other nation. Thus, even though most of the capital invested in South African mines was British or was locally raised, a considerable part of the brain power was American. Americans supplied the expert knowledge when and where it was needed. Upon

---

[4] Jerome L. Babe, *The South African Diamond Fields* (New York, 1872), pp. 27, 32, 56, 105. The inference in Eric Rosenthal's *Stars and Stripes in Africa* (London, 1938), pp. 206, 208, that Babe was associated with Thomas Baines and others in opening the Mashonaland gold fields is not substantiated by Babe's account. He seems to have been in the diamond fields for only about five months and then to have returned to the United States.

[5] In a letter he wrote to a friend on October 3, 1886, J. X. Merriman said, "Your picture of the old Californian panning gold on your stoep is idyllic." See Phyllis Lewsen (ed.), *Selections from the Correspondence of J. X. Merriman, 1870–1890* (Cape Town, 1960), p. 220.

the reports of Americans, capital was raised and shares of stock fell or rose to several times their nominal worth.[6] The significance of the American contribution to the South African gold- and diamond-mining industries therefore lies not in the presence of prospectors but in the fact that so many of the experts who developed the mines and smelters were from the United States.

The naming of a few of the Americans who were prominent in the development of the South African mining industry will suggest the extent of the contribution made by American mining experience. In contrast to the rough-and-ready miner of the frontier and the prospector of the gold-rush days, most of these men were educated and trained in technical colleges in the United States, and several had studied at the Royal Saxon School of Mines, at Freiberg, Saxony, which was then the most advanced mining school in the world. Typically, they came to South Africa with years of experience behind them and with an established reputation in their professional field.

The first noteworthy arrival was Ethelbert Woodford, in 1876. Woodford was exceptional in being an engineer and an authority on mining without benefit of a college degree. By practical experience he became a railway construction engineer, and he seems gradually to have directed his interests into mining. Within a short time after his arrival in South Africa he was appointed town engineer for Kimberley; later he was chief engineer for the mining board. In 1887, after an interval in South America, he returned and became the consultant mining engineer for the Transvaal Republic. In this capacity he drew up the mining code which is still the basis for much of the mining law of South Africa. Woodford gained considerable unpopularity among the mining population by bitterly opposing the efforts of mining adventurers (including many Americans) who sought to escape from the control of the Transvaal government and undermine the republic in order to bring about British annexation.[7]

---

[6] See John Hays Hammond, *Autobiography* (New York, 1935), Vol. I, *passim.*

[7] Patrick Manning, "A Draft: Notes toward a History of American Technical Assistance in Southern Africa, from 1870–1950" (unpublished research paper, California Institute of Technology, 1963 [mimeographed]), pp. 10–11. Woodford was one of the few Americans in South Africa who sided with the Boers during their war with Great Britain. He held a commission from President Steyn of the Orange Free State to enlist American support, which he failed to get.

Important though Woodford's work was, his greatest significance was in being the forerunner—he led and pointed the way for other American mining engineers and technicians who came a few years later and played an even greater part in developing what was to become South Africa's major industry. Among the scores—possibly even hundreds—are four whose contributions are outstanding: Hamilton Smith, James Hennen Jennings, Gardner Williams, and John Hays Hammond.[8]

Hamilton Smith, whose influence was far-reaching, was a Kentuckian of New England ancestry. Like Woodford, he achieved a high place in his profession without academic preparation. His early education was supervised by his grandfather in New England; at the age of fourteen he went to work in the coal mines his father owned in Indiana, to learn about mining engineering problems and accounting, and when barely out of his teens he was a recognized expert in both subjects. In 1869 he went to the Pacific coast and within a few years was probably the world's foremost authority on hydraulics. In California, he attracted the attention of Baron Rothschild, then in America to inspect Rothschild properties, and was engaged by him as a consulting engineer. In that capacity Smith went to El Callao, Venezuela, and there gathered about him a small group of young mining engineers who were destined to leave their mark upon South Africa.

Hamilton Smith did not actually spend much time in Africa. He visited South Africa twice, in 1892 and 1895, but his influence upon subsequent developments in gold production has been immeasurable. It was his report on the potentialities of the South African gold fields, after his first visit, that persuaded the Rothschilds to expand their interests in the country and invest heavily there. The men who developed the industry were men whose training and thought he had influenced deeply.[9]

James Hennen Jennings was one of Hamilton Smith's protégés and, like him, was a native of Kentucky and born to a family with coal-mining interests in Indiana, but his approach to the profession

[8] For other names and a more detailed treatment see *ibid.*, pp. 4–18.

[9] See the article "Hamilton Smith," by Thomas T. Read, in the *Dictionary of American Biography.*

of mining engineer was by the academic route. Jennings attended school in England and graduated from the Lawrence Scientific School of Harvard University. He was associated with Smith in both California and Venezuela and in 1889 was a consulting engineer in London. Within a few months the firm for which he was consultant sent him to South Africa, where he quickly attained a position of influence in the mining industry. When the Transvaal government appointed a commission to inquire into various aspects of mining, Jennings' testimony was said by the chairman to have given the commission a clearer insight into the working of the mines than that of any other witness.[10]

Although most of the American mining experts who applied their training and abilities to the South African mines were concerned with the production of gold, Gardner Fred Williams was a diamond expert. He was a native of Michigan, and having decided on a mining career while still quite young, he became one of the first graduates of the newly established University of California. He went on to the Royal Saxon School of Mines at Freiberg and returned to California for his master's degree. Only after his academic foundation was firmly laid did he commence practical professional work in the mining districts of the Far West and in Mexico. In 1884, upon the recommendation of Hamilton Smith, he was engaged to take charge of some gold-mining properties in the Transvaal. His first sojourn in Africa led directly to acquaintance and association with Cecil Rhodes. This brought him to the attention of the Rothschilds and to the management of the De Beers properties and caused a shift of his interest from gold to diamonds. Williams' seventeen-year management of the De Beers mines helped make them the monolithic center of the world's diamond production.[11]

Probably the most noteworthy and certainly the best known and

---

[10] Evidence and Report of the Industrial Commission of Enquiry (Johannesburg, 1897), passim. Several other Americans also testified before the commission.

[11] A. F. Williams, Some Dreams Come True, pp. 217–238. See also the article "Gardner Williams," by Thomas T. Read, in Dictionary of American Biography, and Gardner F. Williams, "The Genesis of the Diamond," in Annual Report of the Board of Regents of the Smithsonian Institution . . . 1905 (Washington, D.C., 1906), and The Diamond Mines of South Africa: Some Account of Their Rise and Development (New York and London, 1902).

most spectacular of the Americans in South Africa was John Hays Hammond. He was a protégé of Gardner Williams, who had persuaded him to turn down an attractive offer from the mining magnate George Hearst and accept a less lucrative position with the United States Geological Survey for the sake of the experience and knowledge he would thus gain.[12] Hammond did not arrive in South Africa until 1893; he was engaged by Barney Barnato, a London speculator who had amassed a fortune in the mines, to inspect and oversee various properties at the then enormous salary of $50,000 a year. But since Barnato ignored his advice on several occasions, Hammond resigned within a few months and was immediately snapped up by Cecil Rhodes at an even greater salary (rumored to have been $75,000). As one of Rhodes's principal agents and as consulting engineer for Consolidated Gold Fields of South Africa, Hammond had influence second only to that of Rhodes himself in the economic development of South Africa. He hired and fired; he opened and closed mines and plants; and when the interests and ambitions of Rhodes caused him to intervene in South African politics, Hammond became deeply involved in the bitter feud between the Boers and the *Uitlanders* (the foreign residents, chiefly British).

As the richness of the mineral resources of South Africa became apparent to the rest of the world, large numbers of foreigners were attracted to the country. The agrarian-minded Boers of the two independent republics—the Transvaal and the Orange Free State— regarded this influx with deep distrust; they feared Great Britain, and the parents of the vast majority of them had migrated on the Great Trek for the express purpose of escaping from British rule. The Boers had no desire to kill the mining industry, but they were determined to keep political control of the republics in their own hands. At the same time, somewhat shortsightedly, they imposed upon the *Uitlanders* a highly discriminatory system of revenue under which the foreigners paid virtually all the taxes. The mining industry still earned large profits, but some of the British mine and plant operators feared, or professed to fear, that unless drastic steps were taken the Boer farmers would tax the industry out of existence.

The measures taken by the Boers—intended primarily to main-

---

[12] Hammond, *Autobiography*, I, 85–86.

tain their control of the country—conflicted directly with the Rhodes dream of a great British empire in Africa extending from the Cape to Cairo. A head-on collision between the two contrasting and opposed ideals was almost inevitable. During the several years of agitation that preceded the actual break, most of the Americans in South Africa saw only one side of the case and failed to understand that a monopoly by Cecil Rhodes and his group would be as oppressive as the Boer oligarchy. They saw only that the *Uitlanders*, of whom they were a part, were virtually without civic rights, even though they were a clear majority in many areas. Finally, aided and abetted by Rhodes, the foreigners began to plot a revolution. One of the principal conspirators was John Hays Hammond, who maintained that he was doing only what the Americans of 1774 and 1775 had done. Over a stretch of months, he and Gardner Williams smuggled arms and ammunition into the country. Hammond was also instrumental in swinging the support of the Americans in the Transvaal to the revolutionary side. In describing his activities, he wrote:

> I may begin ... with a meeting held by five hundred Americans in Johannesburg ... in December, 1895. What we had met to decide was whether or not we should give our support to a Revolution which was then brewing against the Boer oligarchy.
> Our grievances were so well known that there was no need for me to enlarge upon them; all I had to do was to take the sense of those present—and every class of American was represented—on the single question whether the point had not been reached to which the signers of the Declaration [of Independence] referred.[13]

The plot of the conspirators did not proceed as planned. An armed force consisting mostly of British South Africa Company police, led by Rhodes's close friend, Dr. Leander Starr Jameson (a physician turned miner, soldier, explorer, and administrator), entered the Transvaal from Bechuanaland. These "Raiders" were captured January 2, 1896, at Doornkop, and the movement was nipped in the bud. Hammond, whose part in the conspiracy became known, was arrested, tried by a Boer court-martial, and sentenced to be shot, but

---

[13] *The Truth about the Jameson Raid* (Boston, 1918), pp. 2–4.

the sentence was commuted to the payment of a huge fine and a pledge to abstain from meddling in Transvaal politics.[14]

Among the Americans who had an important part in the development of South African mining one must also mention Louis Seymour, who revolutionized the operation of the diamond mines by his self-winding engines; Leslie Simpson, a graduate of the University of California who, without previous practical experience, established world records for speed and depth in digging mine shafts; George Labram, who attained fame during the Boer War, erected a crushing plant for De Beers, and designed an efficient grease table for catching diamonds in the sorter; and Anthony Robeson, who designed a pulsator for the last stages of diamond sorting. Many other Americans like these helped in various ways to bring South Africa to the important position it has attained in the world's economy.

But the hundreds of Americans in southern Africa in the late nineteenth century were by no means all professional men or highly trained technical specialists. Americans of other kinds, with other skills, were included.

In its rough-riding days the American West produced a redoubtable breed of frontiersmen versed in the arts of the wilderness, of hunting game and finding their way through unknown country— masters in the specialized craft of subduing untamed nature and resisting the attack of red Indian warriors. These skills were equally in demand on the frontiers of South Africa's "Far North," and soon Americans began to make their appearance in the heart of Africa. Adam Renders, a German-American hunter and prospector, was one of these. Apparently he quarreled with and abandoned his family and then "went native" while he hunted elephants in the unknown regions of what is now Rhodesia. There he discovered the ruins of Zimbabwe—as far as is known, the first white man ever to see them —and the prehistoric gold mines in the vicinity.[15]

---

[14] *Ibid.*, pp. 13–31, and *Autobiography*, I, 325–327. See also his wife's account, Natalie Hammond, *A Woman's Part in a Revolution* (London and New York, 1897), *passim*, and the article "John Hays Hammond," in *National Cyclopaedia of American Biography.*

[15] Hammond, *Autobiography*, I, 242; see also L. Sprague de Camp and Catherine C. de Camp, *Ancient Ruins and Archaeology* (Garden City, N. Y., 1964), p. 118.

One of the more picturesque Americans in southern African history was Guillermo Antonio Farini, about whom little is known but who seems to have been a showman, both by instinct and by occupation. He had walked across Niagara Falls on a tightrope; in the 1870's he operated the famous London Aquarium. He first went to South Africa in 1882 to obtain some real Bushmen to take to London—and at least one of those Bushmen came later with Farini to the United States. In 1885 Farini, accompanied by his son, made an exploring and sporting trip into the Kalahari Desert, during which time, if he is to be believed, he discovered the extensive ruins of a prehistoric city. Farini's book about his journey into the Kalahari was one of the first accounts of that remote and unknown region by an eyewitness; his reports on the flora and fauna were acclaimed at the time as important contributions to the world's knowledge of a previously unknown region.[16]

In 1890 Rhodes organized a picked body of young men—the Pioneer Corps—to occupy Mashonaland and take advantage of a concession he and his associates had obtained from the Matabele king, Lobengula. Rhodes instructed Frank Johnson, a young British adventurer to whom he entrusted the details and command of the force, to select only first-class marksmen and horsemen and also to use men representing varied trades and professions. The Pioneer Corps erected a fort in Salisbury, disbanded, and established Rhodes's claim to the vast country that became known as Rhodesia. Soon farmers and ranchers, men, women, and children, flocked into Ma-

---

[16] Guillermo Antonio Farini, *Through the Kalahari Desert: A Narrative of a Journey with Gun, Camera, and Note-book to Lake N'Gami and Back* (London, 1886), *passim*. Only the most fragmentary biographical information on Farini has been found. The authors wish to acknowledge their indebtedness to the Information Division of the New York Public Library for such data as are available. Most authorities on the Kalahari are convinced of the actual existence of the prehistoric city he claimed to have discovered. Several recent attempts have been made to locate it, but without success. See Fay Goldie, *Lost City of the Kalahari: The Farini Story and Reports on Other Expeditions* (Cape Town, 1963). It is obvious from the context of Farini's book that he regarded himself as an American, whatever his ancestry and birth may have been. His work indicates an intelligent, interested observer, as well as a man of courage and common sense. His catholicity of tastes and interests is also indicated by his membership in the Royal Horticultural Society and by the fact that his only other published work is entitled *How to Grow Begonias* (London, 1897).

shonaland. As one of his company commanders and as a key assistant Johnson chose an American who had been in Africa since 1879, Maurice B. Heany (or Heaney—the name was spelled both ways).[17]

What brought Heany to Africa is unknown, but he first became prominent as an officer in the Pioneer Corps and then continued for years thereafter to play a conspicuous part in the affairs of Southern Rhodesia. He and Johnson had become acquainted when they were members of the Bechuanaland Border Police, and later, with a man named Borrow, they formed a business triumvirate that had a marked influence on the economic development of the newly opened territories. In 1885, in one of their first joint enterprises, Heany and Johnson attempted to discover the source of the quills of gold dust which the Africans often used to pay for imported luxuries. Thus, Heany was one of the few white men who had already been in the country to which the Corps was directed and which Rhodes proposed to settle. Heany afterward served with distinction in the Matabele war of 1893 and in the tribal rebellions of 1896. In the abortive Johannesburg revolution of late 1895 (the Jameson Raid) he was the trusted confidential messenger sent by Rhodes with an important message for Jameson. He is said to have been the only raider not captured— he was ungentlemanly enough to violate the tacitly understood rules by shooting his way out through the encircling Boer commandos.[18]

Little is known of Heany's background and his career before coming to Africa. It was widely believed that he had seen considerable service in the Indian wars in the United States, that he was an officer of the U.S. Army, and that he was a Virginian by birth and a cousin of Edgar Allan Poe.[19] Heany spent the remainder of his life

[17] Ian D. Colvin, *The Life of Jameson* (London, 1923), I, 121–125. See also Frank W. F. Johnson, *Great Days: The Autobiography of an Empire Pioneer* (London, 1940), *passim.* It has been said that this famous body of men dispatched by Rhodes to occupy Mashonaland was to Rhodesia what the people of the *Mayflower* were to New England.

[18] See the Heany File in the Southern Rhodesia Archives, Salisbury, and Colvin, *The Life of Jameson,* II, 51–54, 60, 67, 92–93, 118, 162.

[19] Heany is called a "West Pointer" in Reginald Ivan Lovell, *The Struggle for South Africa, 1875–1899: A Study in Economic Imperialism* (New York, 1934), pp. 332–333, but he never attended the United States Military Academy. Further, the authors have been informed by The Adjutant General, Washington, D.C., that there is no record of Heany's ever having served in the United States

in Rhodesia (he died in 1928), living to see the country in which he had pioneered become a modern and civilized state.

The Pioneer Corps included other Americans, among whom was William Harvey Brown. Brown was a young biologist employed in the United States National Museum. On an afternoon in the early autumn of 1889, he was astonished when the director of the Museum, without warning, asked him if he was prepared to sail in a few days for Africa. The government was sending an expedition to Cape Town to observe an eclipse of the sun, and the Museum had been authorized to send a naturalist along to obtain specimens for its collections. The American scientific party was in South Africa while the Pioneer Corps was being formed. Brown and a friend in the American scientific group found the idea of exploring new country most attractive — and Brown, moreover, saw in the Pioneer Corps an opportunity to obtain rare zoological, botanical, and anthropological material for the Museum. With the permission of the chief of the party, the approval of the navy captain in charge of the expedition, and the blessing of the American consul at Cape Town, Brown and his friend enlisted as Pioneers.[20] As a Pioneer, Brown continued to collect and forward scientific material to Washington, and upon the breakup of the Corps he stayed on in Africa. He fought in the Matabele and Mashona rebellions — in the latter he was badly wounded — and did not return to America for almost eight years. His half-brother, from California, helped establish the Botanical Gardens in Salisbury.

Frederick Russell Burnham was probably the best known of all among the Americans who pioneered in Southern Rhodesia. Before coming to Africa, he had already lived an adventurous life that would have satisfied most men. He had been a prospector, a rancher, and a scout with the United States Army in the Apache wars in Arizona. As a scout he surpassed the Indians in their own specialized skills,

Army. For additional information on Heany see William Harvey Brown, *On the South Africa Frontier: The Adventures and Observations of an American in Mashonaland and Matabeleland* (New York, 1899), p. 67, and A. S. Hickman, *Men Who Made Rhodesia: A Register of Those Who Served in the British South Africa Company's Police* (Salisbury, 1960), pp. 30–31.

[20] Brown, *On the South Africa Frontier*, pp. 44–49. It is interesting to note that enlistment in the Pioneer Corps was a private contract. The Corps was a modern revival of an ancient practice — the private army.

having ability at scouting that would have shamed Natty Bumppo or Daniel Boone. Consequently, when he joined the British forces in the Matabele war, he quickly became an important figure. His extraordinary skills and spectacular achievements made him almost a legend. When the Boer republics and the British Empire came to open blows in 1899, the British Commander in Chief, Lord Roberts, invited Burnham to return to Africa to serve as chief scout for the British forces; by special decree he was permitted to accept a commission in the British Army without renouncing his American citizenship.[21] There were not many Englishmen (or Americans), even among the hard-bitten frontiersmen of southern Africa, who could glance at a trail and say approximately how many men and horses had passed, and at what time, or who could sniff a passing breeze and say confidently that an enemy force was so many miles distant. But the legend on Burnham grew, and he was reputedly able to do all these things.

Less dramatic than his achievements as a scout, but more important, was the part Burnham played in discovering some of the copper deposits situated near the Kafue River in Northern Rhodesia. Since the areas of Arizona and northern Mexico where he had prospected were rich in copper, he was able to recognize at once the signs when he saw them. He was led to the discovery by noticing that the slave-wife of a Matabele who was digging a well for him wore a bracelet of native copper. Questioning disclosed that the Matabele had acquired his wife on a raid into a country far to the north. Painfully slow interrogation—for the woman did not speak a language that could readily be understood, even by her husband—revealed how her people obtained the red metal: "Messages repeated back and forth from interpreter to interpreter through four languages brought out these facts: her country was the same number of days march beyond the Great River as it was from Bulawayo to the Zambesi

---

[21] Frederick Russell Burnham, *Scouting on Two Continents* (Garden City, N. Y., 1928), *Taking Chances* (Los Angeles, 1944), *passim*, and his "Remarks," in *Annual Publications of the Historical Society of Southern California*, XIII (1927), Part IV, 334–352. See also Hammond, *Autobiography*, I, 251–253, and Robert S. S. Baden-Powell, *The Matabele Campaign: Being a Narrative of the Campaign in Suppressing the Native Rising in Matabeleland and Mashonaland, 1896* (4th ed.; London, 1901), pp. 70–71, 81–82.

[and] this metal came from ingudines, holes in the ground."[22] The result was that in 1895 Burnham, financed by a group of British and South African capitalists, undertook a systematic exploration for the "holes in the ground" and found where they were.

The adventurous Pioneer Corps was followed by pioneers of a different kind, by civil servants and technicians who laid the foundations of good government without which the country could not have prospered. Once more Americans were among those in the forefront. John Hays Hammond and Gardner Williams drafted Southern Rhodesia's first mining laws, which have since remained substantially unchanged. An American was responsible for laying out the streets and avenues of the capital, Salisbury.

Once a regular administration had been set up, settlers with their families began to come into the country to establish permanent homes. In this process of colonization American enterprise took an important share through its contribution to early transport. Before the construction of the railroad from the Cape into Southern Rhodesia, the familiar American stagecoach, shipped across the seas from the Far West where it had outlived its usefulness, was the de luxe transportation on the African frontier. Cobb and Company, a California firm, is said to be responsible for this particular stroke of business genius.

While the press and people of the United States were largely sympathetic toward the Boers in their disputes with the mighty British Empire, the Americans in South Africa, subjected directly to Boer repression, were almost without exception on the British side. This was clearly manifested in the Boer War (1899-1902), in which many Americans fought on the British side and very few joined the Boer commandos.[23] In the besieged cities or mining camps of Mafeking and Kimberley, the Americans who were cut off from the outside world took active part in the defense. As the Boers closed in on Kimberley, whose defenders were equipped only with small arms and a few pieces of light artillery, Rhodes called one of his American

---

[22] Hammond, *Autobiography*, I, 273–274. Strangely, Burnham, in his published reminiscences and memoirs, makes no mention at all of his exploration of the copper areas.

[23] Cf. Julian Ralph, *An American with Lord Roberts* (New York, 1901), *passim*.

engineers, George Labram, into conference. The result was that Labram commenced work in the De Beers shops on December 27, 1899, and three weeks later a heavy gun of 4.1 caliber began throwing shells to a range of 8,000 yards. Moreover, even before he started to build "Long Cecil," as the gun was nicknamed, Labram had turned the shops into an improvised munitions factory producing ammunition for the light artillery. Without the inventive and mechanical genius of this American, Kimberley might have been forced to surrender.[24]

Although most of the Americans in South Africa had little sympathy with the Boers in the war, a few of them joined the Boer fighting forces; one famous commando unit, the "Irish Brigade," was composed largely of Americans and was commanded by Colonel John Y. Fillmore Blake, a graduate of the United States Military Academy.[25] Blake's brigade took part in all the principal battles of the war (during which Blake himself was wounded) and was not disbanded until the Boer forces finally disintegrated at the end of the war.

---

[24] John Frederick Maurice, *History of the War in South Africa, 1899–1902,* II (London, 1907), 49–50. This is the British official history of the war. See also Louis Creswicke, *South Africa and the Transvaal War,* IV (Edinburgh, n.d.), 21, and Lewis Michell, *The Life of the Rt. Hon. Cecil John Rhodes, 1853–1902* (London, 1910), II, 271–272. According to Michell, Labram's gun was a surprise to the Boers, who retaliated by hauling a 6-inch Creusot gun nicknamed "Long Tom" into position to shell Kimberley. Other writers have stated the converse—that "Long Cecil" was built as a reply to "Long Tom." The latter version seems more probable. Labram was killed on February 9, 1900, by a 100-pound shell from the Boer gun.

[25] John Y. Fillmore Blake, *A West Pointer with the Boers: Personal Narrative of Col. J. Y. F. Blake, Commander of the Irish Brigade* (Boston, 1903), *passim;* Michael Davitt, *The Boers' Fight for Freedom, from the Beginning of Hostilities to the Peace of Pretoria* (New York and London, 1902), pp. 318–327; Charles D. Pierce, *The South African Republics: Souvenir Published for and in Behalf of the Boer Relief Fund* (New York, 1900), pp. 30–31. Blake graduated from West Point in the class of 1880 and spent several years on the frontier as an officer of the 6th Cavalry, United States Army. Upon resigning from the service he went into the railroad business and wound up in South Africa, where he sympathized keenly with the desire of the Boers to preserve their independence from British rule. After the war, he returned to the United States; he died in 1907, at the early age of fifty-one.

The term *brigade,* as used in the Boer forces, bears no reference to a brigade in other armies. Blake's "Irish Brigade" was actually a commando force consisting of about 200 men.

The Boers, as well as the British, availed themselves of American scouting talent and experience. Captain John A. Hassell, a native of New Jersey, organized and commanded a group of Americans as a scouting and reconnaissance force—the American Scouting Corps.[26] Because the Boer side of the war was not well publicized, in spite of efforts to gain American sympathy, nothing can be said as to the actual exploits of Hassell's men, but their services were considered invaluable by the Boer high command.

It seems that a sizable proportion of the Americans on the Boer side were of Irish birth or descent, men whose enmity for Great Britain was traditional and almost hereditary. Certainly, forty volunteers from Chicago who joined the Boer forces and were assimilated into Blake's command were motivated largely by such a sentiment.[27]

The Boer War took place at a time when the American people were becoming increasingly aware of the world outside their own country, and it attracted a good deal of attention in the United States. One of its immediate effects was to stimulate interest in the furnishing of an American hospital ship, in addition to other measures expressive of the humanitarian feelings of the American people. A group of socially prominent American women, led by Lady Randolph Churchill (the mother of Sir Winston Churchill), raised nearly $200,000 and chartered the S.S. *Maine*, which was equipped to succor the sick and wounded of both sides. The surgeons and nursing staff were Americans, and the ship was fitted with the latest and most modern hospital equipment available, including the new marvel, the X ray. Although goods and stores offered by British firms were gratefully accepted by the *Maine* committee, the whole of the subscriptions for the ship came from the American public.[28]

Although mining and the related industries are of extraordinary

---

[26] Davitt, *The Boers' Fight for Freedom*, p. 327; Pierce, *The South African Republics*, p. 22.

[27] Davitt, *The Boers' Fight for Freedom*, p. 325. Possibly these were the members of the "Chicago Hospital Corps," who, according to the New York *Evening Post*, as quoted by Pierce (p. 37), promptly tore off their Red Cross insignia when they neared the front and became part of the Boer fighting forces.

[28] Henry Houghton Beck, *History of South Africa and the Boer-British War* (Philadelphia, 1900), pp. 430–431. It should be noted that the S.S. *Maine* was a converted merchant ship and was unconnected in any way with the U.S.S. *Maine*, destroyed in Havana harbor.

importance in the economy of southern Africa, the region has always been basically agrarian. The American agronomist and horticulturist in southern Africa has been less spectacular in his achievements than the prospector and mining engineer, but his contributions have been solid and extensive. Even more significant than the contributions of individuals is the fact that from America came many of the fruits, vegetables, and other farm products that today are a mainstay of the economy. One needs only to recall that maize, tobacco, and the potato, items which have revolutionized agriculture all over the world, are of American origin.

There is an interesting point regarding American contributions to the mining industry and those to agriculture—the state of California has provided much of the specialized knowledge, skill, and training that went into both. It was in California that most of the American mining experts who took part in the development of South Africa's mines received their initial training and experience; similarly, agricultural skill has come from California, which was recognized as the world's foremost fruit-producing region in the latter part . of the nineteenth century.

The first impact of Americans upon the agriculture of southern Africa occurred in the 1890's, when the phylloxera devastated the vineyards. South Africa had long been famous for its wines, but the industry was threatened with extinction by the ravages of the insect. As in France a few years earlier, the infected stock was dug up and replaced with resistant vines from California, but the vineyardists faced several years of hard times before the imported vines could mature and produce. At this juncture a young American, W. E. Pickstone, entered the scene. He seems to have been related to W. Fox Pickstone, a member of a firm that shipped fruit from South Africa to Great Britain. The American Pickstone was an adventurer at heart and went to Africa in search of excitement in the wars with the tribesmen; but, by education and training in California, he was a skilled horticulturist. He became acquainted with Cecil Rhodes and convinced the magnate that this was an opportune time to buy vast areas of vineyard land cheaply—the owners were glad to sell at any price. Rhodes purchased no less than twenty-five vineyard estates and, under Pickstone's management, had them planted to citrus and other fruits. As in his other enterprises, Rhodes embarked upon fruit raising on a mammoth scale. Shortly after, he augmented the staff by bringing Rees Alfred Davis, an authority on citrus culture, from California. The ultimate result was that South Africa has become one of the leading fruit-producing countries of the world, with annual exports (mostly to Great Britain and the United States) to the value of millions of pounds sterling, carried in fleets of fast refrigerator ships.[29] Other orchard crops too, such as the loquat and pecan nut, and new varieties of old fruits, such as the Satsuma plum and Calimyrna fig, were introduced into South Africa from America.[30]

Southern Rhodesia, before the unilateral declaration of independence by Ian Smith late in 1965, had become the foremost tobacco-producing country of the British Commonwealth. A few early settlers experimented with tobacco, without much success. The tobacco itself was satisfactory, but knowledge of how to cure and season it was lacking. Urged by Earl Grey, who was a director of the British South Africa Company, G. M. Odlum came to the United States and studied all phases and aspects of the tobacco industry. In 1904 he returned to Southern Rhodesia, with several Americans, and applied what he had learned on the plantations and in the warehouses and factories of the United States. With some ups and downs, the cultivation and manufacture of tobacco increased in Southern Rhodesia from that time and tobacco became one of its major economic resources.[31]

In other fields of agriculture Americans have also exerted a degree of influence, particularly among the Africans. American missionaries are believed to have introduced the cultivation of cotton, sugar cane, and rice into South Africa, although the evidence is not conclusive. Certainly the trade and agricultural schools, which were the outgrowth of the need of the early missionaries to establish farms for their own food, have had a marked effect upon tribal life.

[29] The Farrell Shipping Lines of Boston pioneered the sale of South African fruit in the United States.

[30] Rees Alfred Davis, *Citrus-Growing in South Africa: Oranges, Lemons, Naartjes, etc.* (Pretoria, 1919), *Citrus-Growing in South Africa* (Cape Town, 1924), and *Fruit-Growing in South Africa* (Johannesburg, 1928). Davis uses many illustrations and examples of California orchards and fruit processing.

[31] Frank Clements and Edward Harben, *Leaf of Gold: The Story of Rhodesian Tobacco* (London, 1962), pp. 50–53.

CHAPTER 7

Capitalists and Men of God

During the period between the Civil War and the end of the nineteenth century, American relationships with southern Africa, as with the rest of the continent, depended largely on the individual interests of private persons. Political isolationism was so deeply ingrained that the United States government, while endeavoring to keep itself fully informed, followed a policy of remaining strictly aloof from intervention in African affairs. Consequently, it was a very exceptional event when, on December 1, 1889, President Grover Cleveland, the archisolationist who had withdrawn the Congo treaty from the Senate, stated in his annual message to Congress:

> In the summer of 1889 an incident occurred which for a time threatened to interrupt the cordiality of our relations with the Government of Portugal. That Government seized the Delagoa Bay Railway, which was constructed under a concession granted to an American citizen, and at the same time annulled the charter. The concessionary, who had embarked his fortune in the enterprise, having exhausted other means of redress, was compelled to invoke the protection of his Government. Our representations, made coincidentally with those of the British Government, whose subjects were also largely interested, happily resulted in the recognition by Portugal of the propriety of submitting the claim for indemnity, growing out of its action, to arbitration.[1]

The foundation for this statement was laid several years before. On December 22, 1884, the United States Minister at Lisbon wrote in a dispatch to the State Department that the Portuguese government had just granted permission to Colonel Edward McMurdo, an American, to build a railroad from Lourenço Marques, on the Mozambique coast, to the Transvaal frontier. The country to be traversed by the railroad presented few natural difficulties or serious engineering

[1] *Foreign Relations, 1890*, p. viii.

problems. When the work of construction started, it proceeded rapidly. But the project soon became inextricably involved with the Anglo-Boer disputes. Probably, also, Portugal began to fear that it had acted hastily in granting the concession—McMurdo's railroad might provide an excuse for the seizure of Mozambique by the British. Portuguese fears, though not in fact justified, were not allayed by such pronouncements as that made by a British commentator on current events:

> In South Africa . . . our first consideration is the consolidation to their natural limits of the territories to the south of the Zambesi. We must stretch out to the banks of the river; on the North-West we are limited by the German claims; on the North-East every legitimate effort must be made to obtain command of Delagoa Bay and its railway, which, commercially and politically, would render us supreme over all South Africa.[2]

Fear of British seizure of Mozambique was reinforced by the knowledge that most of the bonds for financing the railroad had been sold by McMurdo in London and that the chief engineer in charge of the construction was an Englishman, Sir Thomas Tancred. These factors, combined with vociferous opposition from the authorities of the Transvaal, who were outraged at the prospect of losing revenues accruing from the transportation of goods to the interior, caused Portugal to renege on its concession. On the morning of June 29, 1889, without warning, Portuguese soldiers forcibly seized the property and equipment of the railroad, and Portugal declared the concession canceled. The breach of contract was so flagrant that the United States government shortly felt constrained to take diplomatic action to protect the interests and lawful rights of an American citizen, and Great Britain took similar action. Then, as President Cleveland remarked in his message, Portugal consented to submitting the affair to arbitration.

The Delagoa Bay arbitration case dragged along for ten years. The nearly bankrupt Portuguese government must have regretted many times the impulse that led to the seizure of the railroad. It soon became apparent that the Portuguese legal case was weak and that

---

[2] J. Scott Keltie, "British Interests in Africa," *Contemporary Review*, LIV (1888), 121–122.

Portugal would have to pay a large indemnity. Finally, in 1900, the Swiss arbitration tribunal handed down its decision—against Portugal on all points.[3]

The Delagoa Bay case marks a change, a shift in American relationships with Africa. The latter half of the nineteenth century had seen hundreds of individual Americans contributing each in his own way to the future of Africa. Missionaries, soldiers of fortune and misfortune, farmers, prospectors, explorers, sportsmen, technologists— all had gone to Africa on their own initiative. Edward McMurdo, even though his enterprise was ultimately a failure, marked a new approach. He represented the American capitalist who went to Africa vicariously, through his purchasing and hiring power.

The year 1900 was a turning point for Africa in other ways. At the opening of the nineteenth century, Africa was shrouded in mystery deeper than that over the remotest islands of the South Seas. At the close of the century, much of Africa had been explored by Europeans and, in many cases, by Americans. By 1900 the political boundaries of Africa were established—boundaries that survive almost unchanged today after many African nations have achieved independence. Trade routes were opened, the overseas slave trade was eliminated, and the economic, political, and cultural influences of Europe and America were beginning to make themselves felt. Africa and its peoples had been drawn from relative isolation into the affairs of the world. In this revolution, in this enforced modernization of Africa, Americans without imperial aspirations played a conspicuous part.

The missionaries of the American Board of Commissioners for Foreign Missions—the first American religious representatives in South Africa (1835)—maintained and quietly extended and expanded their efforts until by the close of the nineteenth century they were one of the foremost missionary groups.[4] The Board's activities

---

[3] Malcolm McIlwraith, "The Delagoa Bay Arbitration," *Fortnightly Review,* LXXIV (1900), 413–416, 421–423. See also Philip R. Warhurst, *Anglo-Portuguese Relations in South-Central Africa, 1890–1900* (London, 1962), pp. 113–114.

[4] Johannes du Plessis, *A History of Christian Missions in South Africa* (London and New York, 1911), pp. 303–306. The American Board was originally an interdenominational organization, but soon became exclusively an agency of the Congregational Church, which it remains today.

came to include schools, a theological seminary for educating and training African pastors, and several dispensaries and hospitals. Medical work among the natives received an impetus in 1893 with the arrival of Dr. Burt Nichols Bridgeman, a man who combined high medical skill with an unselfish devotion to the ideals of Christian humanitarianism.[5] Numerous biographical and autobiographical works testify to the vigor of the American Board's handful of missionaries. The foremost authority on missions in South Africa pays this tribute to them: "The translation of the Bible into Zulu . . . was made wholly by various members of the Mission [and] has proved of inestimable benefit to all Christian missions in Natal."[6]

To stress the work of the missionaries of the American Board, because they were pioneers and were the most prominent American religious body in South Africa, is not to detract in any way from the labors and accomplishments of others. Special mention must be made of the work in South Africa of the African Methodist Episcopal Church, one of the leading Negro churches of the United States. In 1896 and 1897 the African Wesleyans (Methodists) broke away from the parent British church and became affiliated with the African Methodist Episcopal Church. In 1898 the union was cemented by the visit of Bishop Henry McNeil Turner, a noted Negro clergyman, who ordained a number of African ministers and took other steps to make the South African churches integral parts of the American body. At the turn of the century, in 1900, another outstanding Negro minister, the Reverend Levi Jenkins Coppin, was designated bishop for South Africa; he further strengthened the position of the African Methodist Episcopal Church by having his episcopal status recognized by the Union of South Africa government. From this beginning, American Negro separatist churches came to influence greatly the movement for independent African churches in the twentieth century.[7]

---

[5] James B. McCord with John S. Douglas, *My Patients Were Zulus* (London, 1951), pp. 41–45. Dr. Bridgeman and his successors were handicapped, oddly enough, by well-meant opposition from a fellow "Board" missionary—a man of dynamic personality who believed in faith healing and succeeded in convincing not only Africans but also some missionaries that disease was merely a punishment for sin and that taking medicine was a sin in itself.

[6] Du Plessis, *A History of Christian Missions in South Africa*, p. 306.

[7] See Levi Jenkins Coppin, *Observations of Persons and Things in South Africa, 1900–1904* (Philadelphia, [1905?]), *passim*.

In 1879 the American Board decided to establish a mission in Portuguese East Africa (as Mozambique was then generally called). The mission was to use Inhambane as a base and then to go to the interior to make contact with the tribes of Gazaland in what became Southern Rhodesia. The Reverend Myron W. Pinkerton, a missionary with almost ten years' experience among the Zulus, arrived at Inhambane in October, 1880, but almost immediately fell victim to a fever and died. The following year his successor, the Reverend Erwin H. Richards, succeeded in reaching the region in which the Board wished to establish its major effort and was received with the greatest cordiality by Umzila, the local king. Umzila was anxious to have missionaries among his people and gave Richards every possible encouragement.

Unfortunately, the Board ran into difficulties in Mozambique. The region was as unhealthy as the deadly western coast, and the local Portuguese authorities were openly hostile. After much trouble the mission finally obtained a tract of land, but the Board's missionaries were forbidden to preach or carry on the usual missionary activities outside its limits. Such handicaps were discouraging and took many months and protracted diplomatic correspondence between Washington and Lisbon to overcome.[8]

Missionaries of the American Board were (as far as available records show) the first Protestant missionaries to work among the Africans of Mozambique. In 1885, acting on a suggestion from the Reverend Erwin H. Richards, a small group of missionaries of the Free Methodist Church arrived at Inhambane and commenced their labors.[9]

The first Methodist Episcopal missionaries arrived at Mozambique in 1890, where they found that Richards, unwilling to abandon the country and migrate to the Board's new mission in Rhodesia, still remained. He changed his denominational allegiance to the Metho-

---

[8] *Foreign Relations, 1884,* pp. 637–640, and *1885,* pp. 646–647. See also Eduardo Moreira, *Portuguese East Africa: A Study of Its Religious Needs* (London and New York, 1936), pp. 20–21.

[9] The Free Methodist Church should not be confused with the African Methodist Episcopal Church or with the Methodist Episcopal Church. The last-named is the denomination usually referred to simply as *Methodists*—a usage which will be followed here.

dists and clung grimly to his post until his death in 1928. From inauspicious beginnings, the Methodist mission in Mozambique grew under Richards' leadership until it became, unquestionably, the most influential Protestant mission in the region. In addition to the usual preaching and efforts at conversion, the Methodist missionaries found time to translate the Bible into the Shitswa language and the New Testament into the Gitonga language.[10]

Meanwhile, in 1888, when the American Board decided to close its mission in Portuguese territory and transfer its work to the interior, its representatives again encountered difficulty. Two missionaries who visited Gungunyana, the son and successor of King Umzila, found that he did not share his father's favorable attitude toward them. His mind had been poisoned against missionaries, and the permission which his father had granted was no longer valid. "Your feet have been too slow in coming," he said curtly, indicating that he wanted nothing more to do with the missionaries.[11] The setback, however, proved to be only temporary. In 1890 Cecil Rhodes's Pioneer Corps entered Mashonaland, and the power, authority, and prestige of the British Empire, albeit indirectly through the British South Africa Company (often referred to as the "Chartered Company"), were cast over the domains of King Gungunyana. Rhodes was anxious to have missionaries work among the African peoples of his newly acquired dominions, and upon learning that the American Board was interested, he offered a tract of land upon which to establish a mission.

In 1892 a party headed by the Reverend George Wilder explored Gazaland and finally selected a site near Mount Selinda, where "the hills and mountains lend grandeur to the scenery and healthfulness of the climate." The site was well within the area pre-empted by Rhodes's company and almost exactly on the spot which he had previously indicated on a map as a suitable location for a mission. For a purely nominal quitrent of £24 per annum, the Board was granted a princely domain of more than 30,000 acres, in two separate tracts.[12]

---

[10] Moreira, *Portuguese East Africa*, pp. 21–22, 81; Erwin H. Richards, "Notes from Inhambane, East Africa," *The Gospel in All Lands* (New York), 1898, p. 415.

[11] Du Plessis, *A History of Christian Missions in South Africa*, p. 307.

[12] *Missionary Herald*, LXXXIX (1893), 25–26, 304.

In June, 1893, the group of missionaries bound for the new mission station arrived at Beira, in Portuguese East Africa, and commenced the journey inland to their new home. Their preparations included huge quantities of supplies and a prefabricated boat made of corrugated iron. The party included a physician, three American and four Zulu missionaries with their wives and families, and a lone female American missionary. The party ascended the Busi River by boat and canoe as far as the falls and cataracts which made further movement by water impossible; they then employed several bearers and traveled the rest of the distance on foot. They had no exciting adventures, but the journey was full of discomfort. The Reverend Fred R. Bunker reported to the Board: "The ladies were introduced to their pioneer experiences by having to sleep on the deck of our sailboat without any mattress. Overhead was stretched the sail of the boat to keep off the dew, which is like rain here, while we were entertained (?) and kept awake all night by the beating of drums and dancing in a kraal nearby."[13] Everybody, including the Zulu assistants, suffered somewhat from fever during the journey, but thanks to increased knowledge of the nature of the disease, no one was seriously affected and there were no casualties. The Reverend Francis Bates, in a letter to the Board written later, remarked, "Everyone full of malaria and quinine—a bitter feeling to the world."[14]

Once at their new station, the group went to work with a will and in a short time constructed a station that would be at least livable until something more permanent could be erected. They built huts with grass roofs and dirt floors—uncomfortable but sufficing to keep off the rain and the dew. The transportation of supplies presented difficulties that were overcome by patience and hard physical labor. Indeed, the Reverend Mr. Bunker had little time for preaching and praying—he was too busy running pack trains from a point a hundred miles distant. He found that "donkey-driving did not leave much time for evangelistic work."[15]

The country was already filling with land-hungry settlers. This fact offered numerous advantages: the mission was easily and quickly

---

[13] *Ibid.*, p. 410.
[14] *Ibid.*, XCI (1895), 190.
[15] *Ibid.*

112

supplied with butter and milk and was able to obtain horses, donkeys, and pigs. But at the same time the missionaries feared the effects upon the Africans of close contact with the newcomers. It became necessary, too, to take immediate possession of the westerly tract allotted to the mission before work was completed on the site where the mission station was to be established. "Squatters" were moving in, and they might become so firmly planted that the mission would forfeit its title. The danger was forestalled, however, and the mission retained ownership of both its allotted tracts without any marked friction with the incoming settlers.

In addition to the purely material activities of building, transporting supplies, and organizing, the little group started energetically upon their major interest. They toured the native villages, preaching and exhorting. Schools were started, although the initial response was discouraging. Dr. W. L. Thompson, the medical member of the group, found his services in demand over a vast area, and regardless of weather or how he felt, he responded whenever he was needed.[16] The feeling of good will the Americans built up among the Africans was such that during the uprising of 1896, when the Mashona joined the Matabele in a frenzied effort to expel the white settlers, the mission and its people stood undisturbed.[17]

The newly opened lands in southern Africa soon attracted the attention of Protestant religious bodies all over Europe and America. In 1894 American Seventh-Day Adventists were granted land by the British South Africa Company and established a mission in Southern Rhodesia, not far from the town of Bulawayo. They were followed in 1898 by American Methodists under the leadership of Bishop Hartzell, who were granted the company's abandoned post at Old Umtali.[18] The Brethren in Christ settled near Bulawayo in 1898.[19]

---

[16] *Ibid.*, pp. 240–241. He reported that in 1894 he responded to no less than 590 professional calls, many of them at a considerable distance.

[17] C. P. Groves, *The Planting of Christianity in Africa*, III (London, 1955), 102.

[18] *Ibid.*, p. 103.

[19] The American Board received nearly 31,000 acres, the Methodists about 10,000 acres, and the Brethren in Christ a little over 3,000 acres. See Per S. Hassing, "The Christian Missions and the British Expansion in Southern Rhodesia, 1888–1923" (unpublished Ph.D. dissertation, American University, 1960), p. 234.

Giving land to British and American missions was part of Rhodes's scheme for Anglo-Saxons to rule the world; it also served to reduce humanitarian criticism of his company in Great Britain. But in addition he may have had a tactical reason for inviting American missionaries. He gave them land along the border of Portuguese East Africa where—it has been suggested, without any direct evidence—he would be able to use them as a diplomatic *cause célèbre* in case of trouble with the Portuguese.[20]

In their schools the American missionaries stressed agriculture and practical training although they did not ignore literary skills.[21] They were accused by settlers of teaching the doctrines of equality and self-government to Africans, but there seems in fact to have been little difference between what European and American missionaries taught.

In the early 1890's a missionary movement in Nyasaland, although not strictly of American origin, became so involved with American Negroes and so dependent upon financial and moral support from the United States that mention of it is not inappropriate. In 1892 a strange, idealistic, visionary, and almost fanatical enthusiast named Joseph Booth arrived in Nyasaland and founded the "Zambesi Industrial Mission." Booth was an Englishman who had spent several years in Australia. Deeply religious from childhood, he questioned the ideas and practices of the established churches. Hence Booth's doctrines were held suspect by more orthodox missionaries; his successes in making converts may possibly have aroused their envy and apprehension. Certainly his ideas of racial equality were disliked by both authorities and settlers, and eventually he was forced from the country. But among his earlier converts was an earnest, intelligent young African named Chilembwe, who achieved an education and ordina-

<hr>

[20] See letter of Dr. W. J. van der Merwe to Per Schioldberg Hassing, August 30, 1958, *ibid.*, p. 237.

[21] After 1900 the two outstanding mission schools that emphasized a program of practical training were run by the Americans G. A. Roberts and Emory Alvord. Subsequent to 1926, when he became Director of Native Agriculture, Alvord started a veritable revolution in African agriculture by introducing agricultural demonstration work. See the Alvord File in the Southern Rhodesia Archives, Salisbury, and articles by Alvord in *NADA* (the Southern Rhodesia Department Annual), No. 2, 1929, and *Bulletin Agricole du Congo Belge,* September-December, 1949.

tion in the United States. Chilembwe, on his return to Nyasaland, established a mission upon the same lines as that founded by Booth —an industrial mission in which Africans were trained in arts and crafts as well as taught Christianity. Later, however, Chilembwe and his mission, with American Negro missionaries among the staff, became the focus of a violent revolution which, unhappily, had to be suppressed by force.[22]

American missionaries were also active in other parts of southern Africa during the latter part of the nineteenth century. Religious bodies interested in promoting missions in Africa were attracted to the vast Portuguese domain of Angola, which was practically a blank on the mission map. In 1880 three missionaries of the American Board (one of them a Negro) arrived in Angola and took the first steps in establishing a mission at Bailunda, deep in the interior, among the Ovimbundu people of the Benguela highlands.[23] The mission expanded, and the future seemed to be promising, but troubles started in 1884 when the local king suddenly ordered the missionaries out of his realm. Since the government of Portugal had approved the establishment of the mission, the matter called for diplomatic intervention by the United States government. Correspondence between Washington and Lisbon dragged along for more than two years. Apparently the expulsion was prompted by an unscrupulous local Portuguese trader, Eduardo Braga, who saw a threat to his trade and profits if the missionaries became too influential; the Portuguese governor of Benguela, for private reasons, appears also to have been interested in getting rid of the strangers. The king (or Sobo) of Bailunda enjoyed a considerable degree of autonomy under Portuguese rule, and when Braga persuaded him that the Americans were fugitives from justice in their own country and meant no good to him and his subjects, the king acted promptly. The culmination of the affair,

---

[22] See George Shepperson and Thomas Price, *Independent African: John Chilembwe and the Origins, Setting, and Significance of the Nyasaland Native Rising of 1915* (Edinburgh, 1958). Chilembwe and the rebellion of 1915 are to be discussed in more detail in a later installment of this study, dealing with the period after 1900 (in preparation).

[23] James Duffy, *Portuguese Africa* (Cambridge, Mass., 1959), p. 124; Kenneth Scott Latourette, *The Great Century in . . . Africa (A History of the Expansion of Christianity*, Vol. V; New York and London, 1943), p. 399.

late in 1885, was an apologetic letter from the king to the Reverend W. H. Sanders; in this he explained why he had felt compelled to act as he did, and then he added, "But I have orders from the governor at Loanda to take you back." The king was willing to return the missionaries' confiscated property and effects for a consideration, and he naïvely included in his letter a demand for a monthly payment from them. Beyond this, the published records are silent, but it is a reasonable assumption that the missionaries recovered their personal effects without the payment of a ransom and did not pay a monthly bribe to the somewhat avaricious potentate.[24] In spite of these early difficulties, the mission of the American Board in Angola expanded and prospered and within a few years was one of the most influential missions in that part of the world.

Angola was a promising field. In 1885, the American Board missionaries were followed by a group of Americans representing the Methodist Episcopal Church and led by Bishop William Taylor, who had been designated as the Methodist Missionary Bishop of All Africa the year preceding.[25] Taylor, who was somewhat of a visionary, was convinced that missions should, and could, be self-supporting. He succeeded in convincing the laymen and clergy of his church of the soundness of his ideas and was directed by the General Conference of 1884 to found, wherever possible, new missions in Africa on the self-supporting plan. He arrived at Loanda in 1885 with thirty men and women dedicated to establishing missions in Angola and maintaining themselves and the missions by their own efforts. Spurred on by Taylor's exuberant personality and by their own enthusiasm, the Methodists established five stations in Angola. But they soon found that the good bishop's ideas were completely unrealistic—to support themselves, build and maintain missions, and conduct evan-

---

[24] *Foreign Affairs, 1884,* pp. 634–636, and *1885,* pp. 631–634, 641, 643–648.

[25] Taylor was an enthusiast—a natural evangelist—who had labored as a street-corner preacher in San Francisco and had spent several years, on leave of absence from his Conference, as a voluntary missionary in Canada and Australia in the 1850's and 1860's. From Australia, the illness of his young son had led him to the healthful climate of South Africa, and his attention became fixed upon the missionary needs of the vast African continent. Believing that his God directed all events, he felt that his sojourn in Africa because of his child's illness was a manifestation of a call from God to evangelical labors in that quarter. See his *Christian Adventures in South Africa* (New York, 1879), pp. 1–11.

gelical labors simultaneously was impossible. "They all endeavored to make ends meet by engaging in commerce, cattle-raising, working at a trade, or farming generally," said an optimistic account by Héli Chatelaine, a member of the group, in the London *Christian* of March 9, 1888, and he described the efforts of the devoted men and women to keep body and soul together. At Loanda they established a school, which seems to have been highly successful, although it "would not have kept the teachers without the addition of income from private lessons in languages." At a station which the bishop established at a village about three hundred miles from the coast, the missionaries set up a farm. "A large tract of land was cleared, well laid out, ploughed and planted, and houses built on it," but the reporter commented, "As farming in a new country is rich in disappointments, it has not yet paid sufficiently to support the station." One member of the party was "earning his support by collecting medicinal plants for the Congo State."[26]

In spite of the optimism of the Methodist group, Bishop Taylor's experiment was doomed to failure. At almost the same time as Chatelaine's account, the *Northwestern Christian Advocate* quoted one of the missionaries as saying that the destitution among some of them was pitiable. Moreover, he noted that when they could obtain remunerative work, it was often of a kind they could not conscientiously perform, such as repairing stills or keeping accounts for unscrupulous traders.[27]

Bishop Taylor continued to maintain his enthusiasm, but when he was succeeded by Bishop Joseph C. Hartzell in 1896, the Methodist missions in Angola were on the edge of extinction. The church's Missionary Society took over the financial responsibilities, placing their missionaries on a salary basis, like the missionaries of other churches. The Methodist missionaries in Angola (and in other parts of Africa as well) were then free to devote themselves to evangelism and did not have to expend their time and energy in a struggle for survival. The Methodist missions in Angola began at last to gather strength

---

[26] Quoted in "Bishop Taylor's Missions in Angola," *The Gospel in All Lands*, 1888, pp. 216–218. See also Johannes du Plessis, *The Evangelisation of Pagan Africa* (Cape Town, 1930), pp. 232–233.

[27] Quoted in "Bishop Taylor's Missions in Angola," p. 219.

and grow; Bishop Taylor's stout optimism had its indirect reward.[28]

Héli Chatelaine, whose report on the pioneer group in Angola has been quoted, was a naturalized American citizen, Swiss by birth, gifted with remarkable ability as a linguist. His function in the group was to acquire sufficient knowledge of the native languages to instruct the missionaries, so that they might preach to and converse with the Africans in their own idiom. Chatelaine's activities were handicapped by the necessities of the self-supporting scheme, but still he managed to prepare a dictionary and grammar of the Kimbundu language, translate a gospel into that tongue, and make a scientific study of some of the folklore of Angola. In 1897 he resigned from the Methodist mission and established an independent and nondenominational endeavor, the *Mission philafricaine,* devoted to teaching the Africans the useful arts as well as the principles of the Christian religion.[29]

Concurrent with the efforts of missionaries from the United States to establish themselves and preach the Gospel on the continent of Africa were those of American missionaries on the island of Madagascar. Although never as prominent in religious work on the island as were missionaries of other nationalities, they aided and reinforced activities already established. In 1888 the American Lutheran Missionary Society, which seems to have been founded and maintained largely by Norwegian immigrants to the United States, sent representatives to Madagascar, and a mission was established with headquarters at Fort-Dauphin. Two years later another body of American Lutherans, the Lutheran Board of Missions, founded a mission at Manasoa, in the province of Tullear. According to available information no other American missionary bodies were represented in Madagascar, though the missions of the Society of Friends (Quakers) in the country included a number of Americans in their personnel.[30]

The part played in Africa during the latter half of the nineteenth century by Americans, or by men so closely associated with the

---

[28] Du Plessis, *The Evangelisation of Pagan Africa,* p. 233. See also Bishop Taylor's own optimistic statement quoted in *The Gospel in All Lands,* 1889, pp. 478–479.

[29] Du Plessis, *The Evangelisation of Pagan Africa,* pp. 234–235.

[30] James Sibree, *Fifty Years in Madagascar: Personal Experiences of Mission Life and Work* (London, 1924), pp. 301, 321.

United States that they may reasonably be considered Americans, was not negligible. Nevertheless, it has been largely ignored or overlooked not only by European historians but by American historians as well. There are works on missionary activities which do not mention a single American missionary or missionary agency. Although no one studying the history of Africa can ignore Stanley, few have ever heard of Arthur Donaldson Smith or Mason A. Shufeldt. And the role of the American mining experts in developing the fabulous mineral riches of South Africa has too long remained unpublicized. It is not claimed that the part taken by the United States and its citizens in the African drama was as significant or as spectacular as that of the nations which pre-empted vast colonial empires in Africa. But the role of Americans in the great African continent has been important, and American contributions to the development of Africa have been many and lasting.

Bibliography

I. *Unpublished Materials*

Alvord, Emory. File in Southern Rhodesia Archives, Salisbury.

Booth, Alan R. "Americans in South Africa, 1784–1870." Unpublished Ph.D. dissertation, Boston University, 1964. 338 pp.

Bowen, Thomas Jefferson. The Thomas Jefferson Bowen Papers. MSS held by the Southern Baptist Convention Historical Commission, Nashville, Tenn.

Brooks, George E. "American Legitimate Trade with West Africa, 1789–1914." Unpublished Ph.D. dissertation, Boston University, 1962. 281 pp.

Harr, Wilber Christian. "The Negro as an American Protestant Missionary in Africa." Unpublished Ph.D. dissertation, University of Chicago Divinity School, 1945. 214 pp.

Hassing, Per S. "The Christian Missions and the British Expansion in Southern Rhodesia, 1888–1923." Unpublished Ph.D. dissertation, American University, 1960. 391 pp.

Heany, Maurice B. File in Southern Rhodesia Archives, Salisbury.

Howard, Lawrence Cabot. "American Involvement in Africa South of the Sahara, 1800–1860." Unpublished Ph.D. dissertation, Harvard University, 1956. 347 pp.

Manning, Patrick. "A Draft: Notes toward a History of American Technical Assistance in Southern Africa, from 1870–1950." Unpublished research paper, California Institute of Technology, 1963. Mimeographed. 57 pp.

Mohun, Richard D. The Richard Dorsey Mohun Papers, National Archives, Washington, D.C.

Phillips, Clifton Jackson. "Protestant America and the Pagan World: The First Half Century of the American Board of Commissioners for Foreign Missions." Unpublished Ph.D. dissertation, Harvard University, 1954. 359 pp.

Sanford, Henry Shelton. The Henry Shelton Sanford Papers, Sanford Memorial Library, Sanford, Fla.

Shufeldt, Robert W. The Robert W. Shufeldt Papers, 1864–1884, Naval Historical Foundation Collection, on deposit in the Library of Congress.

Van de Velde, Lieven. The Papers of Lieut. Lieven Van de Velde, University of Oregon Library, Eugene, Oregon.

II. *Published Materials*

A. Articles

Bennett, Norman Robert. "Americans in Zanzibar, 1865–1915," *Essex Institute Historical Collections*, XCVIII (1962), 36–61.

"Bishop Taylor's Missions in Angola," *The Gospel in All Lands* (New York), 1888, pp. 216–218.

Burnham, Frederick Russell. "Remarks," *Annual Publications of the Historical Society of Southern California*, XIII (1927), 334–352.

"The Congo Commission," *Bradstreet's*, X (1884), 146.

"The Egyptian Campaign in Abyssinia, from the Notes of a Staff Officer," *Blackwood's Edinburgh Magazine*, CXXII (1877), 26–39. Reprinted in *Littell's Living Age*, Ser. 5, XIX (1877), 278–286.

Eilts, Hermann Frederick. "Ahmad Bin Na'aman's Mission to the United States in 1840: The Voyage of *Al-Sultanah* to New York City," *Essex Institute Historical Collections*, XCVIII (1962), 218–277.

Keltie, J. Scott. "British Interests in Africa," *Contemporary Review*, LIV (1888), 115–125.

McIlwraith, Malcolm. "The Delagoa Bay Arbitration," *Fortnightly Review*, LXXIV (1900), 410–429.

Mohun, Richard Dorsey. "The Death of Emin Pasha," *Century Magazine*, XLIX (1894–1895), 591–598.

Rantoul, Robert S. "The Port of Salem," *Essex Institute Historical Collections*, X (1869), 53–72.

Richards, Erwin H. "Notes from Inhambane, East Africa," *The Gospel in All Lands* (New York), 1898, p. 415.

Shufeldt, Mason A. "La Question Malagache [*sic*]," *The United Service*, IX (1883), 453–460.

———. "To, about, and across Madagascar," *The United Service*, XII (January-June, 1885), 1, 506, 691, and XIII (July-December, 1885), 79, 203. (In five installments.)

Weeks, Clelia L. "Zanzibar," *Harper's Magazine*, XXXVIII (1868–1869), 306–318.

Williams, Gardner F. "The Genesis of the Diamond," in *Annual Report of the Board of Regents of the Smithsonian Institution . . . for the Year Ending June 30, 1905* (Washington, D.C., 1906), pp. 193–210.

B. Books and Pamphlets

Anderson, Benjamin J. K. *Narrative of a Journey to Musardu, the Capital of the Western Mandingoes*. New York: S. W. Green, 1870. 118 pp.

Angove, John. *In the Early Days: The Reminiscences of Pioneer Life on the South African Diamond Fields*. Kimberley and Johannesburg: Handel House, 1910. 213 pp.

Anstey, Roger. *Britain and the Congo in the Nineteenth Century*. Oxford: Clarendon Press, 1962. 260 pp.

Babe, Jerome L. *The South African Diamond Fields*. New York: D. Wesley, 1872. 105 pp.

Baden-Powell, Robert Stephenson Smyth. *The Matabele Campaign: Being a Narrative of the Campaign in Suppressing the Native Rising in Matabeleland and Mashonaland, 1896*. 4th ed. London: Methuen, 1901. 500 pp.

Barclay, Wade Crawford. *Early American Methodism, 1769–1844*. New York: The Board of Missions and Church Extension of the Methodist Church, 1949–1950. 2 vols. These two volumes together form Part I of the four-volume series, *History of Methodist Missions*.

Beck, Henry Houghton. *History of South Africa and the Boer-British War*. Philadelphia: Globe Bible Publishing Co., 1900. 496 pp.

Belmont, Perry. *An American Democrat: The Recollections of Perry Belmont*. 2d ed. New York: Columbia University Press, 1941. 729 pp.

Blake, John Y. Fillmore. *A West Pointer with the Boers: Personal Narrative of Col. J. Y. F. Blake, Commander of the Irish Brigade.* Boston: Angel Guardian Press, 1903. 314 pp.

Boulger, Demetrius Charles de Kavanagh. *The Congo State; or, The Growth of Civilization in Central Africa.* London: W. Thacker, 1898. 418 pp.

————. *The Reign of Leopold II, King of the Belgians and Founder of the Congo State, 1865–1909.* 2 vols. London: Ardenne, 1925.

Bourne, Henry Richard Fox. *Civilization in Congoland: A Story of International Wrong-Doing.* London: P. S. King and Son, 1903. 311 pp.

Brady, Cyrus Townsend, Jr. *Commerce and Conquest in East Africa, with Particular Reference to the Salem Trade with Zanzibar.* Salem, Mass.: Essex Institute, 1950. 245 pp.

Brown, William Harvey. *On the South African Frontier: The Adventures and Observations of an American in Mashonaland and Matabeleland.* New York: Scribner's, 1899. 430 pp.

Burnham, Frederick Russell. *Scouting on Two Continents.* Garden City, N.Y.: Doubleday, Page, 1928. 370 pp.

————. *Taking Chances.* Los Angeles: Haynes Corp., 1944. 293 pp.

Chaillé-Long, Charles. *My Life in Four Continents.* 2 vols. London: Hutchinson, 1912.

Clements, Frank, and Edward Harben. *Leaf of Gold: The Story of Rhodesian Tobacco.* London: Methuen, 1962. 223 pp.

Colston, R. E. *Rapport sur les régions centrales et nordiques du Kordofán.* Cairo, 1875.

Colvin, Ian Duncan. *The Life of Jameson.* 2 vols. London: Arnold, 1923.

Coppin, Levi Jenkins. *Observations of Persons and Things in South Africa, 1900–1904.* 2 vols. Philadelphia: A.M.E. Book Concern, [1905?].

Cornet, René J. *Sommaire de l'histoire du Congo belge.* Brussels: L. Cuypers, 1948. 59 pp.

Cornevin, Robert. *Histoire du Congo (Léopoldville).* Paris: Editions Berger-Levrault, 1963. 366 pp.

Coupland, Reginald. *The Exploitation of East Africa, 1856–1890: The Slave Trade and the Scramble.* London: Faber and Faber, 1939. 507 pp.

Crabitès, Pierre. *Americans in the Egyptian Army.* London: Routledge, 1938. 277 pp.

Creswicke, Louis. *South Africa and the Transvaal War.* 7 vols. Edinburgh: T. C. and E. C. Jack, 1900–[1903].

Crowe, Sybil E. *The Berlin West African Conference, 1884–1885.* London, New York, and Toronto: Longmans, Green, 1942. 249 pp.

Davis, Rees Alfred. *Citrus-Growing in South Africa.* Cape Town: Specialty Press of South Africa, 1924. 309 pp.

————. *Citrus-Growing in South Africa: Oranges, Lemons, Naartjes, etc.* Pretoria: Government Printing and Stationery Office, 1919. 66 pp.

————. *Fruit-Growing in South Africa.* Johannesburg: Central News Agency, 1928. 532 pp.

Davitt, Michael. *The Boers' Fight for Freedom, from the Beginning of Hostilities to the Peace of Pretoria.* New York and London, 1902. 603 pp.

De Camp, L. Sprague, and Catherine C. de Camp. *Ancient Ruins and Archaeology*. Garden City, N.Y.: Doubleday, 1964. 294 pp.

Dicey, Edward. *The Story of the Khedivate*. New York: Scribner's, 1902. 539 pp.

Duffy, James. *Portuguese Africa*. Cambridge: Harvard University Press, 1959. 389 pp.

Du Plessis, Johannes. *The Evangelisation of Pagan Africa*. Cape Town: J. C. Juta, 1930. 408 pp.

————. *A History of Christian Missions in South Africa*. London and New York: Longmans, Green, 1911. 494 pp.

English, George Bethune. *A Narrative of the Expedition to Dongola and Sennar under the Command of His Excellence Ismael Pasha, Undertaken by Order of His Highness Mehemmed Ali Pasha, Viceroy of Egypt; by an American in the Service of the Viceroy*. Boston: Wells & Lilly, 1823. 177 pp.

Evidence and Report of the Industrial Commission of Enquiry. Johannesburg, 1897. 747 pp.

Farini, Guillermo Antonio. *Through the Kalahari Desert: A Narrative of a Journey with Gun, Camera, and Note-book to Lake N'Gami and Back*. London: S. Low, 1886. 475 pp.

Farwell, Byron. *The Man Who Presumed: A Biography of Henry M. Stanley*. New York: Holt, 1957. 334 pp.

Fechet, Oscar E. *Journal of the March of an Expedition in Nubia between Assouan and Abouhamed . . . 1873*. Cairo: Egyptian General Staff, 1878.

Ferguson, John H. *American Diplomacy and the Boer War*. Philadelphia: University of Pennsylvania Press, 1939. 240 pp.

Goldie, Fay. *Lost City of the Kalahari: The Farini Story and Reports on Other Expeditions*. Cape Town: A. A. Balkema, 1963. 136 pp.

Gray, James. *Payable Gold: An Intimate Record of the History of the Discovery of the Payable Witwatersrand Goldfields and of Johannesburg in 1886 and 1887*. [Johannesburg]: Central News Agency, 1937. 286 pp.

Groves, Charles Pelham. *The Planting of Christianity in Africa*. 4 vols. London: Lutterworth Press, 1948–1958.

Hammond, John Hays. *The Autobiography of John Hays Hammond*. 2 vols. New York: Farrar & Rinehart, 1935.

————. *The Truth about the Jameson Raid*. Boston: Marshall Jones, 1918. 50 pp.

Hammond, Natalie. *A Woman's Part in a Revolution*. London and New York: Longmans, Green, 1897. 144 pp.

Hargreaves, John D. *Prelude to the Partition of West Africa*. London: Macmillan, 1963. 383 pp.

Heard, William Henry. *The Bright Side of African Life*. Philadelphia: A.M.E. Publishing House, 1898. 184 pp.

Hesseltine, William B., and Hazel C. Wolf. *The Blue and the Gray on the Nile*. Chicago: University of Chicago Press, 1961. 290 pp.

Hickman, A. S. *Men Who Made Rhodesia: A Register of Those Who Served in the British South Africa Company's Police*. Salisbury: British South Africa Company, 1960. 462 pp.

Hill, George Birkbeck (ed.). *Colonel Gordon in Central Africa, 1874–1879.* 2d ed. London: De la Rue, 1884. 456 pp.

Hird, Frank. *H. M. Stanley: The Authorized Life.* London: Stanley Paul, 1935. 320 pp.

Imhoff, Alexander J. *The Life of Rev. Morris Officer, A.M.* Dayton, Ohio: United Brethren Publishing House, 1876. 464 pp.

Johnson, Frank William Frederick. *Great Days: The Autobiography of an Empire Pioneer.* London: Bell, 1940. 366 pp.

Latourette, Kenneth Scott. *The Great Century in the Americas, Australasia, and Africa, A.D. 1800–A.D. 1914.* (*A History of the Expansion of Christianity,* Vol V.) New York and London: Harper, 1943. 526 pp.

Leveque, Robert J. *Le Congo belge: Son histoire.* Brussels, Editions du Marais, n.d. 101 pp.

Lewsen, Phyllis (ed.). *Selections from the Correspondence of J. X. Merriman, 1870–1890.* Cape Town: Van Riebeeck Society, 1960. 303 pp.

Liebrechts, Charles. *Congo, suite à mes souvenirs d'Afrique: Vingt années à l'administration centrale de l'Etat Indépendant du Congo (1889–1908).* Brussels: Office de Publicité, 1920. 336 pp.

Loring, William Wing. *A Confederate Soldier in Egypt.* New York: Dodd, Mead, 1884. 450 pp.

Lovell, Reginald Ivan. *The Struggle for South Africa, 1875–1899: A Study in Economic Imperialism.* New York: Macmillian, 1934. 438 pp.

McCord, James Bennett, with John Scott Douglas. *My Patients Were Zulus.* London: Muller, 1951. 256 pp.

Marcosson, Isaac F. *An African Adventure.* New York and London: Lane, 1921. 288 pp.

Mason, Alexander M. *Report on a Reconnaissance of Lake Albert.* (Proceedings of the Royal Geographical Society, Vol. XXII.) London, 1878.

Maurice, Albert (ed.). *H. M. Stanley: Unpublished Letters.* New York: Philosophical Library, 1957. 183 pp.

Maurice, John Frederick. *History of the War in South Africa, 1899–1902.* 4 vols. London: Hurst and Blackett, 1906–1910.

Michell, Lewis. *The Life of the Rt. Hon. Cecil John Rhodes, 1853–1902.* 2 vols. London: Arnold, 1910.

Moore, Ernst D. *Ivory, Scourge of Africa.* New York and London: Harper, 1931. 256 pp.

Moreira, Eduardo. *Portuguese East Africa: A Study of Its Religious Needs.* London and New York: World Dominion Press, 1936. 104 pp.

Pearce, F. B. *Zanzibar, the Island Metropolis of Eastern Africa.* London: T. F. Unwin, 1920. 431 pp.

Pierce, Charles D. *The South African Republics: Souvenir Published for and in Behalf of the Boer Relief Fund.* New York, 1900. 48 pp.

Prout, Henry G. *General Report on the Province of Kordofan.* Cairo: Egyptian General Staff, 1877.

Ralph, Julian. *An American with Lord Roberts.* New York: Stokes, 1901. 314 pp.

Reeves, Jesse Siddall. *The International Beginnings of the Congo Free State.* (Johns Hopkins University Studies in Historical and Political Science, Ser. 12, XI XII.) Baltimore: Johns Hopkins Press, 1894. 95 pp.

Richardson, Nathaniel R. *Liberia's Past and Present.* London: Diplomatic Press, 1959. 348 pp.

Rosenthal, Eric. *Stars and Stripes in Africa.* London: Routledge, 1938. 306 pp.

Ross, Emory. *Out of Africa.* New York: Friendship Press, 1936. 216 pp.

Sheppard, William Henry. *Pioneers in Congo.* Louisville, Ky.: Pentecostal Publishing Co., n.d. 157 pp.

Shepperson, George, and Thomas Price. *Independent African: John Chilembwe and the Origins, Setting, and Significance of the Nyasaland Native Rising of 1915.* Edinburgh: University Press, 1958. 564 pp.

Sibree, James. *Fifty Years in Madagascar: Personal Experience of Mission Life and Work.* London: G. Allen & Unwin, 1924. 359 pp.

Slade, Ruth M. *English-speaking Missions in the Congo Independent State (1878–1908).* Brussels: Académie Royale des Sciences Coloniales, 1959. 408 pp.

Smith, Arthur Donaldson. *Through Unknown African Countries: The First Expedition from Somaliland to Lake Lamu.* London and New York: Arnold, 1897. 471 pp.

Stanley, Henry Morton. *The Congo and the Founding of Its Free State: A Story of Work and Exploration.* 2 vols. New York: Harper, 1885.

———. *How I Found Livingstone: Travels, Adventures, and Discoveries in Central Africa, Including Four Months' Residence with Dr. Livingstone.* London: Sampson Low, 1873. 736 pp.

———. *In Darkest Africa; or, The Quest, Rescue, and Retreat of Emin, Governor of Equatoria.* 2 vols. New York: Scribner, 1890.

———. *Through the Dark Continent; or, The Sources of the Nile, around the Great Lakes of Equatorial Africa, and down the Livingstone River to the Atlantic Ocean.* 2 vols. New York: Harper, 1878.

Stevens, Thomas. *Africa as Seen by Thomas Stevens and the Hawk-Eye.* Boston: Blair Camera Co., 1890. 25 pp.

———. *Scouting for Stanley in East Africa.* New York: Cassell Publishing Co., 1890. 288 pp.

Stewart, Thomas McCants. *Liberia, the Americo-African Republic: Being Some Impressions of the Climate, Resources, and People, Resulting from Personal Observations and Experiences in West Africa.* New York: E. O. Jenkins Sons, 1886. 107 pp.

Stockwell, G. S. *The Republic of Liberia: Its Geography, Climate, Soil and Productions, with a History of Its Early Settlements.* New York: A. S. Barnes, 1868. 299 pp.

Taylor, William. *Christian Adventures in South Africa.* New York: Nelson and Phillips, 1879. 557 pp.

Wack, Henry Wellington. *The Story of the Congo Free State: Social, Political, and Economic Aspects of the Belgian System of Government in Central Africa.* New York and London: Putnam, 1905. 634 pp.

Warhurst, Philip R. *Anglo-Portuguese Relations in South-Central Africa, 1890–1900.* London: Longmans, 1962. 169 pp.

125

Williams, Alpheus F. *Some Dreams Come True: Being a Sheaf of Stories Leading up to the Discovery of Copper, Diamonds and Gold in Southern Africa, and of the Pioneers Who Took Part in the Excitement of Those Early Days.* Cape Town: H. B. Timmins, [1948]. 590 pp.

Williams, Gardner Fred. *The Diamond Mines of South Africa: Some Account of Their Rise and Development.* New York and London: Macmillan, 1902. 681 pp.

Wilson, Charles Morrow. *Liberia.* New York: W. Sloane Associates, 1947. 226 pp.

Younger, Edward. *John A. Kasson: Politics and Diplomacy from Lincoln to McKinley.* Iowa City, Iowa: State Historical Society of Iowa, 1955. 450 pp.

C. United States Government Documents

Congress. House. *Letter from the Secretary of the Interior . . . as to Contracts for Returning and Subsistence of Captured Africans.* 37th Cong., 2d sess., H.R. Exec. Doc. 12. Washington, 1862.

————. ————. *Message of the President, December 1, 1862.* 37th Cong., 3d sess., H.R. Exec. Doc. 1. Washington, 1863.

————. ————. *Participation of the United States in the Congo Conference.* 48th Cong., 2d sess., H.R. Report 2655. Washington, 1885.

————. ————. *Report on Commercial Relations of the United States with All Foreign Nations.* 34th Cong., 1st sess., H.R. Exec. Doc. 47. Washington, 1857.

————. Senate. *Letter of the Secretary of State, Transmitting a Report on the Commercial Relations of the United States with Foreign Countries for the Year Ended September 30, 1862.* 37th Cong., 3d sess., S. Exec. Doc. Washington, 1863.

————. ————. "Message of the President, December 3, 1861," *Senate Executive Document 1.* 37th Cong., 2d sess. Washington, 1861.

————. ————. *Report of the Secretary of State Relative to Affairs of the Independent State of the Congo.* 49th Cong., 1st sess., S. Exec. Doc. 196. Washington, 1886.

————. ————. "Report of the Secretary of the Interior," *Senate Executive Document 1.* 37th Cong., 2d sess. Washington, 1861.

Congressional Directory. 48th Cong., 1st sess. Washington, 1884.

Department of State. *Commercial Relations of the United States with Foreign Countries.* Washington, 1865–1900.

————. *Papers Relating to the Foreign Relations of the United States.* Washington, 1865–1900.

Department of the Navy. *Annual Report of the Secretary of the Navy for the Fiscal Year Ending June 30, 1880.* Washington, 1880.

D. Reference Works

Dictionary of American Biography. 20 vols. New York: Scribner's, 1928–1936.

National Cyclopaedia of American Biography. 46 vols. New York: James T. White & Co., 1893–1963.

Index

Vizetelly, Frank, 82

Warner, D. B., 30
Webb, Francis Ropes, 69–70, 72
Webb, John F., 69, 72
Webster-Ashburton Treaty, 14–15
West Africa, 20, 22–23, 24, 25–26
Wilberforce, William, 13

Wilder, George, 111
Williams, Gardner, 92, 93, 94, 95, 101
Wilson, Commander Byron, 71–72
Woermann, A., 38
Wolseley, Lord, 44
Woodford, Ethelbert, 91–92

Zanzibar, 19, 43, 45, 67–74, 81, 82